CONVERSATIONS

ON

LIBERALISM AND THE CHURCH.

BY

O. A. BROWNSON, L. L. D.

———•••———

WIPF & STOCK · Eugene, Oregon

Wipf and Stock Publishers
199 W 8th Ave, Suite 3
Eugene, OR 97401

Conversations on Liberalism and the Church
By Brownson, O. A.
ISBN 13: 978-1-60608-676-6
Publication date 5/8/2009
Previously published by D. & J. Sadlier & Co., 1870

PREFACE.

THIS little volume must speak for itself. The Conversations turn on questions of the day and the hour, and taken as a whole they form a passable defence of the Church against the objections urged in the name of Liberalism and Progress, or so-called Modern Civilization. They are not purely imaginary, but such as I have really had time and again with the enemies of the Church, who object to her principally on political and social grounds.

The form of the work has been adopted for my own convenience and that of the reader, and I hope will not be found objectionable. The doctrine is, I believe, rigidly orthodox. I have sought neither to offend the world nor to conciliate it. I do not believe in making concessions of what is not mine to concede. I have explained the teachings of the Church where they conflict with the spirit of the age, but I have not sought to conform them to that spirit. The Church was instituted by our Lord to govern the world according to the Divine Reason and Will, not to be governed by it. These Conversations are respectfully dedicated to all who have or seek after Christian Truth, by

THE AUTHOR.

ELIZABETH, N. J., April, 1869.

CONTENTS.

	PAGE.
PREFACE,	3
CHAPTER I.,	7
CHAPTER II.,	20
CHAPTER III.,	33
CHAPTER IV.,	52
CHAPTER V.,	65
CHAPTER VI.,	78
CHAPTER VII.,	89
CHAPTER VIII.,	104
CHAPTER IX.,	119
CHAPTER X.,	132
CHAPTER XI.,	149
CHAPTER XII.,	160
CHAPTER XIII.,	173

LIBERALISM AND THE CHURCH.

CHAPTER I.

DURING the intense heat of the summer days of 1868, I was ordered by my physicians to try the virtues of a newly-discovered mineral spring, in a distant State, which was beginning to acquire considerable reputation. The number of visitors was not large, for it had not yet become a fashionable watering-place, and few, except such as were really in pursuit of health, or at least desirous of recruiting their exhausted energies, visited it. They were chiefly overworked lawyers, merchants, traders, editors, and ministers of religion, who required relaxation from labor and rest, with freedom from their ordinary cares and anxieties.

I belonged to none of those classes. I had no profession, no occupation, and, with a moderate but competent estate inherited from my grandfather, I was free to follow my own tastes and pleasures. I was past middle age, unmarried, and had no near relatives dependent on me for support or protection. I was as free as a man can be in this world; had originally an excellent constitution, which I had not always respected, and was now suffering from early imprudences and ills incident to idleness and good living. My real complaint was, that I had nothing to do, or to take up my attention; so, as I said, my physicians ordered me to try the waters of the new Spa. I cannot say much for the waters, but the journey I was forced to make, the change of scenery, the pure mountain air, and the intellectual and intelligent company I found had their effect, and, after an absence of a few months, I returned to my home completely renovated in body, and with my mind engaged with a subject not unlikely to occupy it the rest of my life.

While at the spring, around which had sprung up a small village called Springdale, consisting of an unfinished meeting-house, one or two boarding-houses, and a large hotel, I formed the acquaintance of several gentlemen whose conversation interested me much. Among them were two who particularly attracted my attention. One, many years the elder, was apparently a minister or a priest, with a quiet and unobtrusive manner, evidently a man of foreign birth and education, but speaking English as if it had been his native tongue. He must have been at least threescore and ten, but his form was erect and his eye undimmed, his natural strength unabated, and his voice unbroken, sweet, melodious, and sympathetic. He had for me a singular attraction, and I felt prepossessed in his favor at first sight. The other was an active, energetic man, under middle age, well made, with dark hair, heavy brows, and sharp, restless, black eyes. His manner was not rude, but brisk and a little imperious, and he spoke always in a bold, confident tone, from which no appeal might be taken. He gave always his opinion promptly and unhesitatingly on any and every subject that came up, and seemed to have left no subject in law, politics, theology, literature, science, or art on which he was not competent to pass a final judgment. It is hardly necessary to add that he was the chief editor of a leading metropolitan journal.

The two gentlemen were much together, and seemed to take no little interest in each other, although I could not discover that any topic was ever broached between them on which they did not disagree very essentially. Their conversation, or rather their discussion, attracted me as a listener, at first as drawing off my thoughts from myself, and afterwards by the interest it awakened in the subjects on which it chiefly turned, and I seldom failed to hear it. Other guests seemed as much attracted as myself, and whenever we saw them seated under the shade of the old maple-trees left standing near our hotel, we formed a ring around them, and sat and listened in silence.

The editor was a man of our times, animated by the spirit of the age, and a firm believer in our glorious nineteenth century. "The great objection, Father," said he one day to the priest, as I soon learned he was, "to the Church, is her unprogressive character. She fails to keep religion up with the times, refuses to advance with modern society, and the world goes on without her."

"Whither?" quietly asked the priest.

"Whither? Why, on its progressive march."

"Do you mean that the Church herself is not progressive, or that she opposes progress in individuals and society?"

"Both. The Church is stationary, remains what she was in the Dark Ages, does her best to keep society back where it was a thousand years ago, and to prevent the human race from taking a step forward."

"There is, I suppose, no doubt of that?"

"Not the least."

"Is it not possible for the Church to remain immovable herself, and yet be very progressive in her influence on individuals and society generally?"

"To aid progress the Church must be herself progressive."

"You see, then, neither argument nor wit in Dr. Johnson's reply to the learned butcher who gave it as his opinion that to criticize a great poet, one should himself be a great poet: 'Nonsense, sir! as well say he who kills fat oxen should himself be fat.' I have always thought differently. Progress is motion; and if I have not forgotten what my professor of mechanics taught me, there is no motion possible without something at rest. Motion requires a mover, and the mover cannot move unless it is itself immovable. A man cannot make any progress if he stands on a movable foundation, as you may see in the case of the poor fellow in the treadmill. Archimedes, in order to move the world, demanded a whereon to rest the fulcrum of his lever outside of the world he proposed to move. The Church, if herself movable or progressive, could not aid either social or individual progress; she would simply change with the changes going on around her, and could neither aid nor control them."

"But, Reverend Father, you overlook the fact that it is precisely in herself that progress is most needed. She teaches the same dogmas and claims the same authority over the mind, the heart, and the conscience in this enlightened age, and in this free republic, that she did in the barbarous ages under feudalism, and what she teaches and claims ceases to be in harmony with men's convictions, or their sense of their own rights and dignity."

"The Church, then, you think, in order to be able to serve the world, should not govern it, but suffer herself to be governed by it, and take care to teach it only what it already believes and holds? This is a very good principle, no doubt, for a journalist, who seeks only a wide circulation for his journal, but do you think our Lord acted on it? Did he find the convictions of the world he came to redeem and save in harmony with his doctrines and claims? If so, how came the Jews to reject him and crucify him between two thieves? Did the Apostles teach only such doctrines and put forth only such claims as were in harmony with the sentiments and convictions of their age? Why, then, did their age make martyrs of them? How much would our Lord and his Apostles or Christians during the martyr ages have done to advance the world, think you, if they had only echoed its opinions, approved its superstitions, and suffered themselves to be dictated to and governed by it? Would you have the Church conform to the world and be a time-server? For my part, I have always held the Church to be instituted to teach and govern all men and nations in all things spiritual, and not to be taught and governed by them."

"That is precisely my objection. The Church places herself above the people, assumes to be wiser than they, claims the right to govern them, and therefore denies their sovereignty."

"Their sovereignty in spirituals, certainly, in temporals, as against the inherent sovereignty of kings or nobilities, not at all. But you are losing sight of your objection. You objected to the Church that she is not progressive, teaches now the same doctrines and makes the same claims that she taught and made in the Dark Ages. Be it so. Are those doctrines false and unfounded? If so, you should have objected their falsity and invalidity. If true and just, how can she depart from them without departing from truth and justice? Your objection is not well taken, unless you hold that truth and justice are variable, and change from age to age and from nation to nation, or as men's views of them change."

"Your Church is undemocratic, and places herself above the people, allows the people no voice in her administration, or in determining the doctrines to be taught."

"All in good time, my dear Mr. Editor. Just at present, pray tell me if truth is variable—one thing to-day and another to-morrow?"

"Truth, like everything else, is progressive."

"Do you mean that the truth itself is progressive, or that our knowledge of it is progressive?"

"Progress is the law of the universe."

"Of the created universe, in relation to the end for which it exists, be it so; but do you pretend that the Creator of the universe is progressive?"

"Why not?"

"Because he is Being in its plentitude, and could not be Creator if he were not. Progress is going from imperfection towards perfection, and is predicable only of an existence that depends on another for its being, and that has not yet actualized all the possibilities of its nature. God is independent, needs only himself, is eternally perfect, is, as say the theologians, most pure act, in whose nature there are and can be no potentialities or unactualized possibilities, consequently in him there is no room for progress. To suppose him progressive, is to suppose him a creature, imperfect, dependent, movable ; and to suppose him, or to suppose truth movable or progressive, is to fall into the error of those whom Plato calls the ancestors of the Greeks, who held that all things are in a perpetual flux and reflux, and that there is nothing fixed or stable. We should thus deny progress in the very act of asserting it."

"How so ?"

"If all things are in a perpetual flux and reflux, there is for things neither beginning nor end, and without both no progress is possible. Progress is proceeding, morally as well as physically, from a starting-point to an end or goal. It means literally stepping forward, that is, action from a fixed point to a fixed point; remove the points, and no progress is conceivable. Before you can pronounce a man progressive, you must know that he has a beginning as well as an end; so truth must have a beginning and an end, in order to be progressive. You must say the same of God. Will you say now that God is progressive?"

"I pretend not that. He is without variableness, or shadow of turning. But truth is not God."

"What is it then?"

"Nobody can say. We only know what it is in relation to us, or what seems to us to be true. We never know the absolute; our knowledge stops with the relative. Things may be true to you, and not to me, in one age or country, and not in another. I have no doubt that the doctrines and claims of the Church were very admissible in the Dark Ages, and that they then served the cause of progress, of religion, of civilization. They were then in harmony with the age, and were true and useful; but that does not imply that they are either now."

"Beware, my dear friend, of the treadmill. It is painful to be compelled to stand on the wheel, to keep stepping from morning to evening and never get a step forward. But will you tell me what doctrines or claims of the Church were true and useful in the Dark Ages that are false and hurtful now?"

"We need not descend to particulars. There is no doubt that the Church, for several centuries after the fall of the Roman Empire of the West, was a powerful and beneficent institution, and exerted a happy influence in promoting civilization. She saved from utter destruction the arts, the literature, and the sciences of the old Græco-Roman world; she softened the manners, and infused the sentiments of humanity into the hearts of the rude Barbarians that issued forth from the forests of Germany and seated themselves on the ruins of the Empire, by preaching to them the doctrine of brotherly love, by presenting them as the model of all excellence the meek and lowly Jesus, going about doing good when he had not where to lay his head, and dying on the cross for the redemption of his enemies, whom with his latest breath he forgave and prayed for. But having done that work, she is now only in the way of further progress."

"The preservation of the arts, literature, and sciences of the old Græco-Roman world could do nothing to advance civilization beyond the point reached by Greece and Rome, and therefore can hardly be said to have done anything for progress. Was it by what she retained of the old civilization that she tamed and humanized the Barbarians, or by what she added of her own? You say what she added by her doctrine of brotherly love, or the brotherhood of the race, and the example of the meek and lowly Jesus, presented as the model of excellence. Well, are these things less true and useful now than they were then? Or is there any doctrine the Church teaches, or any claim she puts forth to govern or discipline her own children, true and useful in relation to past ages or nations, that is not equally so now?"

"Whether the Church was or was not relatively true and useful in those ages that knew no better than to believe her dogmas, practise her worship, and submit to her despotic authority, it is certain that she is hostile to all modern civilization, and the chief obstacle to progress, or the organization of society according to the laws of nature."

Here I thought the able editor rather evaded than met the home question of the venerable priest. Though all the listeners were against the priest and on the side of the metropolitan editor, their looks indicated that they wished him to state specifically and distinctly what in the Church was true and useful at one time that can be false and hurtful at another. They all believed that the Church had corrupted the faith, and buried it beneath a mass of unmeaning ceremonies, degrading superstitions, and human or satanic inventions, but they could not concede that truth itself is variable, or that the good effected was effected by anything not always and everywhere true and useful.

CHAPTER II.

"You say, my dear Editor," replied the priest, "that the Church is hostile to modern civilization, and an obstacle to individual and social progress. One thing at a time, if you please. I presume that you will agree with me that before we can decide what favors or retards progress, we must determine what is or is not progress. Will you tell me what you understand by progress?"

"Progress is leaving the dead past and moving forward towards the living future. It is a continual melioration or advance from the imperfect towards the perfect. It is the continual enlargement of the quantity of our being, or the realization of the possibilities of our nature."

"I would strike out from your definition the enlargement of the quantity of our being, because our being is not in ourselves, but in God, in whom 'we live and move and are,' and therefore can neither be increased nor diminished, since God is being in its plenitude, and self-existent. The literal or etymological meaning of the word is, as I before said, 'a stepping forward.' When taken in a figurative sense, as we are now taking it, you very well define it to be an advance from the imperfect towards the perfect. But before we can assert progress, whether of the individual or of society, we must know that the perfect of each really exists, though not yet attained to, or that there really is an end in which the progress terminates because, when it is attained, the perfect is reached; and before we can say this or that favors or retards progress, we must know what this end or this perfect is, or, in other words, in what the perfection of society and the individual man consists."

"The perfection consists in the complete realization of the possibilities of nature."

"But how am I to determine what are the possibilities of my individual and social nature, or whether I am realizing them or not? Progress implies imperfection, incompleteness, for what is perfect, complete, is not and cannot be progressive, since there are in it no unrealized possibilities. Imperfection implies perfection, which is its complement or fulfilment. If there is no perfect, there can be no imperfect. How am I to determine what this perfect is, or what is the true end of man and society, so as to be able to assert what is or is not progress?"

"It is not necessary to determine what it is. One has but to follow nature, for nature points directly to it."

"You mean that nature of itself goes instinctively, by the force of its own inherent laws, to its end?"

"Such is my meaning."

"What is the use, then, of intelligence and moral effort? and wherein is there, then, any specific difference between man and the elemental forces of nature, between gratitude and gravitation, between virtue and vice, a moral act and an immoral act? Man would then act only as the winds and waves, storms and tempests, or as the thunderbolt that rives the oak—at best only as the beasts that perish. Call you this asserting the rights and dignity of man?"

"No; I recognize in man a moral nature."

"Right. But a moral nature acts for an end—*propter finem*, not simply to an end—*ad finem*, and therefore from intelligence and will, or reason. Then we must know the end, for we cannot will what we do not apprehend. Now the Church, my worthy young friend, teaches us what is this end, the true and last end of man, and also what is the end of society—points out the way we must go to attain to either, furnishes the means needed to gain it, and urges us by motives terrible as hell and as sweet and attractive as heaven to struggle for it. How, then, can you say that she is an obstacle to progress?"

"She may not oppose what she calls progress, but she opposes what this age understands by progress."

"That is possible. There are many things in which she and this age do not agree. But does she oppose anything that *you* call progress?"

"She opposes popular education, the diffusion of intelligence among the people, is hostile to popular liberty, upholds tyrants and tyranny, and resists everywhere with all her power the introduction and establishment of popular government."

"May it not be that you mean one thing by these terms, and she another?"

"She opposes the emancipation of the people from ignorance and superstition, and their instruction in their rights and the means of asserting and maintaining them."

"Does the Church oppose the emancipation of the people from what she holds to be ignorance and superstition, or their instruction in what she acknowledges to be their rights and dignity?"

"You asked me to say in what respect she opposes what I call progress. I call progress the enlightenment of the people, their emancipation by the diffusion of intelligence from ignorance and superstition, and their instruction in respect to their rights."

"Why not add to rights, *duties*? Men have duties us well as rights. Is that a true instruction which teaches men their rights, but says nothing as to their duties?"

"Men's duties grow out of their rights, and if duly instructed as to their rights, they can hardly remain ignorant of their duties."

"It would, perhaps, be more just to say men's rights grow out of their duties, but neither form of expression is exact. Men's duties grow out of their several relations, and their rights are simply their freedom to discharge their duties, or to act according to these relations, without any let or hindrance. Man has relations to his Creator, to his neighbor or society, and to the external world. Out of these relations grow three classes of duties—duties to God, duties to our neighbor, and duties to the state or civil society that has charge of material interests, that is, religious, social, and political duties. In regard to these three classes of duties and their correlative rights, which cover the whole field of human activity, it shows great ignorance or great untruthfulness to pretend that the Church opposes the instruction or enlightenment of the people. Has she not the Sacrament of Orders, and does she not educate and ordain a numerous class, as numerous a class as possible, of priests, one, and that not the least, of whose functions is to teach all ranks and conditions of men, even the poor of this world, whom the great neglect and the rich oppress, these three classes of rights and duties? Does she not found or encourage the founding of schools, academies, colleges, universities, for the education of the youth of all classes in the several sciences and the liberal arts, or general and special secular learning? Has she not religious orders and congregations of both sexes whose special vocation it is to teach your sons and daughters? Has she not founded nearly all the great universities of Europe, such as Oxford, Cambridge, Paris, Bologna, Padua, Salamanca, Alcalà?"

"Yet she opposes all efforts to emancipate the people from superstition, and in her schools and colleges she teaches ignorance, and repulses science."

"That she opposes the emancipation of the people from superstition, is a mistake. I am a priest, received my education partly in Spain and partly in Rome; I have travelled over most European countries, and over nearly every State in the American Union, and wherever I have been, whether in schools or seminaries, I have found her making it the duty of her priests and professors to do their best to free the people from all superstitious notions and practices. You cannot take up a single one of her catechisms for the instruction of children and youth that does not teach them to avoid superstition and all approach to it."

"That is all very well; but her own doctrines and practices are superstitious. What else is the doctrine that a little water sprinkled or poured on the head of an infant, and a few magical words mumbled by the priest at the same time, can regenerate the soul, and translate it into the kingdom of Christ?"

"Nothing instituted or commanded by our Lord can be superstition. He instituted the Sacrament of Baptism, commanded his Apostles to go and teach all nations, baptizing them in the name of the Father, and of the Son, and of the Holy Ghost, and has declared that unless a man be born again of *water* and the Holy Ghost, he cannot enter into the kingdom of God. The Church neither believes nor teaches that the water or the words regenerate: they are only the outward or visible sacrament, through which the regenerating grace of the Holy Ghost is communicated."

"The Church seeks to keep the people in ignorance, on the principle that ignorance is the mother of devotion."

"I have already shown you the contrary. But of what does she seek to keep the people ignorant? Is it of theology, the queen of the sciences? Is it of philosophy, of ethics, politics? Is it of astronomy, mathematics, mechanics, chemistry, electricity, cosmology, zoology, biology, physiology, philology, geology, botany, geography, history natural, civil, or ecclesiastical? I am aware of no prohibition against the study of any of these sciences. The Church may not accept all the inductions or theories that many scientists are too prone to put forth as science, but she opposes no well-authenticated facts, and no well-established science. Indeed, my dear Editor, the Church is so far from holding that ignorance is the mother of devotion, that she regards it as her worst enemy, and never ceases to combat it with all her energy."

"She is hostile to liberty, and opposes every effort made to advance it."

"The word *liberty* is much used, and much abused. It is taken in many senses, and not seldom in no definite sense at all. Men differ widely among themselves as to what is or is not true liberty, and no less as to the proper means of gaining or of preserving it. In some of the senses in which the word is taken the Church certainly opposes it, in others she approves and defends it. She opposes liberty in the sense of license or freedom from all law or authority; for she holds, what all experience teaches, that liberty in any good sense cannot exist without law to define and protect it, and that law is inconceivable without a law-giver, and null without authority that has the right to enact and enforce it. But, on the other hand, she has always condemned tyranny and oppression, and at times gone so far as to excommunicate and depose the tyrant, and to absolve his subjects from their oath of allegiance. Nearly all her doctors agree in teaching that the tyranny of the prince absolves the subject, though they uniformly condemn sedition, conspiracy, insurrection, or rebellion against the state as grievous sins as well as political crimes. The Church loves, blesses, and protects liberty as she understands it, and her understanding of it, at the very lowest, is as likely to be just as is that of modern secret societies, who, in the name of liberty, practise the most outrageous tyranny over their members."

"Yet the Reverend Father will not deny that the Church is opposed to popular or democratic government, and fulminates her anathemas against all who are laboring to introduce and establish democracy in Europe."

"I have observed, my dear friend, that your free-thinking gentlemen, who claim to be enlightened above ordinary mortals, are very neglectful of the categories, that they mix up the incongruous in the same sentence, make assertions that may be one-tenth true and nine-tenths false, and then conclude the truth of their whole assertion, as if all the incongruous matter jumbled together in it pertained to the same category. They probably thus deceive themselves, and certainly deceive others. You should mind the categories, and be always careful to define your terms. The Church never opposes, but always supports, and requires her children to support, popular democratic government, when and where it is the legal order. She has never condemned democracy, nor erected any particular form or constitution of government into an article of faith, or a Catholic dogma. She requires all her children to obey the law, and to be loyal to the constitution of their country, as long as it remains the legal government, whatever its form. She forbids them, whatever the regimen under which they live, to be seditious or turbulent citizens, or to do anything contrary to Christian charity. She teaches that unjust laws are violences rather than laws, and do not bind the conscience, and that always and everywhere we are to obey God rather than men; but that to avoid the danger of turbulence or sedition, from a just regard for the peace and order of society, love to our neighbor or our country, we may often be bound to obey even unjust laws, if they only require us to suffer wrong. Yet if they require us to do wrong, or what God forbids, we are by no means to obey them, but to suffer martyrdom rather, as did the early Christians under the heathen emperors. What the Church really opposes, anathematizes, if you will, is neither popular government nor legal efforts to introduce and establish it, but efforts to introduce and establish it by unlawful means, by the crimes of sedition, insurrection, rebellion, or violent revolution—crimes which strike at all law, all civil justice, and render all orderly and stable government impracticable. She holds it as wrong to conspire to overthrow the existing government by violence in the name of the people, as in the name of monarchy or aristocracy."

This, I confess, struck me as a fair view of the case. If we hold that a certain portion of the people of a nation may, when they choose, conspire against the legally existing government, and by rebellion and civil war overthrow it, we take from law its sacredness and inviolability, and render all government, except that of mere brute force, impossible. The people have, undoubtedly, the right to reform, amend, modify, or change their institutions as they see proper, but only by such means as the existing law or constitution authorizes or does not prohibit, as under our American system.

I could never understand why sedition, insurrection, rebellion, should be less criminal under or for a democracy than under or for a monarchy. Obedience to law is as much a duty under a republican as under any other form of government. If not, on what ground can the General government pretend to justify the war it lately waged for the suppression of the revolt of the Southern States, especially since those States did not defend their secession from the Union on the ground of the "sacred right of insurrection," or revolution, as Lafayette calls it. In nearly all cases, the act of insurrection or rebellion against the national authority is the act of a disappointed or turbulent minority, making itself formidable by secret combinations and underground operations. Their aim is to make their will override that of the majority. Their leaders seldom attain to power without proving themselves detestable tyrants, cruel, greedy, and selfish monsters. But the imperturbable editor proceeded on the maxim of all successful journalism, "whether convinced or not, never own that you are in the wrong."

CHAPTER III.

"THEN again," went on the able editor, as if the priest had said nothing, "your Church is undeniably at war with all modern civilization. You see it in the Papal Encyclical of 1864, with its appended Syllabus of condemned errors. All those liberal-minded and enlightened Catholics who partake somewhat of the spirit of the nineteenth century, disapprove the retrograde policy of the *oscurantisti*, and seek to effect a reconciliation between the Church and modern ideas, or between her and our advanced and ever advancing civilization, are, if not absolutely under the ban of the ecclesiastical authorities, looked upon with distrust, held to be dangerous men, and false, if not to the doctrines, at least to the spirit of the Church. To call a member of your Church a liberal, is little less damaging to his character than to call him a heretic. Every advance in modern civilization has been effected not only without the aid of the Church, but in spite of her most strenuous resistance."

"Mind the categories, my dear Editor. Such things are a little vague, and must be defined before one can say precisely what they are or are not. Will you tell me precisely what you understand, first, by civilization, and second, by modern civilization?"

"Civilization is one of those terms which are more easily understood than defined. It needs no defining."

"To lend itself to vague declamation, certainly not. But you and I are not declaiming; we are endeavoring to look seriously and dispassionately at things as they are. Words are nothing except in their meaning, and their meaning is worthless, or worse, if not clear, distinct, fixed, and definite. Civilization is a word of recent coinage, and its meaning is vague, loose, and floating. It hardly means the same thing to any two minds. It was at first a court term, and a civilized person meant one who had the manners and breeding of the court; it was next used to designate, by way of extension, the town-bred, or, as Shakespeare calls it, 'inland-bred,' as distinguished from the country-bred, or rustics and clowns; but gradually, without losing entirely its relation to polite or urbane manners, it has come, in most modern languages, to mean the political and social order which stands opposed to barbarism, and includes ideas, manners, polity, government, laws, arts, sciences, and religion. Its essential meaning may be determined either by ascertaining the essential element of barbarism to which it is directly opposed, or by analyzing the nations generally recognized as civilized, and ascertaining their essential and distinctive principle.

"The essence or the distinctive principle of barbarism, I take it," continued the priest, "is the domination of will directed by passion, the distinctive or essential principle of civilization, as I understand it, is the government of will directed by reason, or power obeying the dictates of justice. The barbarian state is that in which the government is force exercised by the lawless will, the caprice, the unrestrained passions of the chief, who holds the power as his own indefeasible right, and uses it at and for his own pleasure alone. In the civilized state the supreme political power vests in the nation; and the chief magistrate, be he called king, emperor, or president, and all subordinate officers, hold their power as a trust to be exercised for the public or common good. All despotic states are therefore to be classed as barbarian, and all civilized states as republican in principle. The distinction between barbarism and civilization, is simply the distinction between despotism and liberty, or republicanism, taking the word *republican* in its radical or etymological sense, correctly translated by your English word *commonwealth*. Now when and where does the Church oppose, or ever has opposed civilization in the sense I have defined?"

"Your definition is not broad enough to include all that is commonly understood by civilization. We commonly include in it refinement of manners, mental and moral culture, the fine arts, and the sciences."

"My definition does not exclude them, but those are all to be found in a greater or less degree in both ancient and modern nations not usually, if ever, counted among civilized nations. All I have pretended to do is to give the distinctive character or mark of civilization, and that is liberty, the supremacy of law, or power directed and controlled by justice or reason, not by arbitrary will directed and controlled by passion. But be this as it may, we have already seen that the Church opposes none of the things which you pretend my definition does not include. She refined and softened the manners and humanized the sentiments of the Barbarians who overthrew the Roman Empire, as you yourself have admitted, and I have challenged you to name the science she opposes. I have shown you that she favors education and general intelligence by all the means in her power, and even you will not pretend that she has not been the great patron of the fine arts. If you should attempt to do it, her grand cathedrals, which the nations that have renounced her communion cannot even copy, and the magnificent pictures that adorn her churches, would soon reduce you to silence. The fact is, and everybody knows it, that all the civilized nations of Europe, indeed, all the civilized nations now existing on the face of the globe, have received their civilization from her, and owe it to the patient and often misunderstood labors of her pontiffs, her priests, her religious, and her faithful people, giving form and expression to the faith and charity living and working in them. Pray tell me what there is, then, in modern civilization, that she opposes?"

"She opposes all that is peculiar to it, and constitutes its glory."

"The distinguishing feature of modern civilization, if we take what is positive in it, is the application of the discoveries of science to the mechanic and productive arts. Has she opposed this application? Does she condemn the use of the steam-engine, the spinning-jenny and spinning-mule, or the power-loom, the steamboat, the railroad, the locomotive, or the lightning telegraph; mowing, reaping, threshing, or winnowing machines; steam-ploughs, iron-clads, and the like?"

"The Pope for a long time resisted, I believe, the construction of railroads in the Pontifical States."

"As temporal sovereign he may have done so, and he doubtless had his reasons, good or bad; but has he ever condemned the construction of railroads and the use of locomotives as prohibited by the Christian faith, or declared them forbidden by the law of God?"

"I am not aware that he has."

"Then he has not opposed them as head of the Church; and what he may or may not have opposed as head of the state is nothing to me, who am not his temporal subject. Since railroads, steamboats, and the various applications of science to the invention and construction of labor-saving machinery have been introduced, and the modern world is adjusted to them, we could not well do without them, and it would be a calamity to be deprived of them; but there are grave thinkers who greatly doubt if real civilization has been advanced by them, or if the world gets on any better with than it did without them. They have completely changed the face of the industrial world, to some extent the mutual relations of capital and labor, and vastly increased the power of production; but that they have made it easier for a poor man to earn his living, or added anything to the real happiness or well-being of the people, is not so certain. Under the new system, the rich as a class grow richer, and the poor as a class grow poorer. The small home industries of the olden time give way to large industries, in which capital, as necessary to introduce machinery, counts for more, and labor for less. Wages may be nominally higher, but are less in proportion to the wants of the laborer."

"You do not agree with the political economists, who tell us a very different story."

"The political economists consider man only as a producing, distributing, and consuming machine, and seek only to get the greatest possible supply with the greatest possible demand. I, by my profession, if not by my sympathy with my fellow-men, am led to look upon man as having a sentient, intellectual, and moral nature, and I seek for him the greatest possible sum of virtue and happiness. It is not likely, then, that the political economists and I should think alike. It adds not to the well-being of the poor that the aggregate wealth of a nation increases, if they are all the time growing poorer, and find it every day more difficult to supply their wants, or to obtain by honest industry their bread. Under the new system, it may be that wealth increases, but the tendency in the great industrial nations is to concentrate it in fewer hands, or in huge overgrown corporations, which in your country are stronger than the government, and control, not always the elections, but the legislative assemblies, both state and national.

"I was taught," continued the priest, "that to make a man happy we should study not to increase his stores, but to diminish his desires. The political economists study to increase a man's desires, and to develop new wants in him, in order to increase as much as possible consumption, which, in turn, will increase the demand, and the increased demand will stimulate increased production. The demand creates the supply, and the supply stimulates consumption, which, in turn, creates an increased demand.

This, if I understand it, is the essence of your modern science of political economy. But what is the gain to the laborer?"

"He is better fed, better clothed, better lodged than he was under the old system. He can satisfy more wants, and the more wants one satisfies, the more he enjoys."

"The more wants one has that he is unable to satisfy, the more he suffers. A man's happiness does not consist in the number of wants satisfied, but in having no wants unsatisfied. It may well be conceded that if the laboring classes were thrown back into the condition in which they were in the Middle Ages, or even in the sixteenth century, they would be far more wretched than they are now; but that is not the question. Were their means of satisfaction less, in proportion to their actual wants, then than they are now, in proportion to their present actual wants? No doubt more wants may now be satisfied, but that is nothing, if there is a proportionate increase of wants that are not and cannot be satisfied."

"Do you contend that the proportion between the wants and the means of satisfying them has been diminished under the wonderful development of commerce and industry since the beginning of the present century?"

"Between what were the wants of the workingmen in former times, and their present means of satisfying them, no; but between their present wants and the means of supplying them, yes. This is an age of forgetfulness. You seem to forget that no longer ago than 1848 nearly all European society was convulsed by the loud demand for what was then called the 'right to labor,' the right to gain one's bread by the sweat of one's face. Thousands, millions even, of men in the great industrial and commercial nations, able and willing to work, were standing idle, gaunt and grim, because there was no work to be had. The labor market was overstocked; supply had outrun the demand. The demand for labor depends on the state of the markets throughout the world, and a surplus of labor is the normal state in all your great industrial and commercial centres. Were the whole productive force at the command of industry employed to its full extent, more could be produced in any one year than could be disposed of to the actual consumer in any four years, as I am told by those who profess to know, and consequently the operatives are either thrown out of employment or compelled to work on short time for what is equivalent to three out of every four years.

Hence the frequency of distress in manufacturing districts, which finds relief only in public or private charity. Various expedients are suggested by political economists, and tried by governments, but as yet with indifferent success. A favorite measure with one class is what is called protection, or a tax imposed on the importation of foreign productions for the protection and encouragement of our own. But this does not help the operative class; for its only effect is to increase the profits of the capital employed in the industries protected, and these enhanced profits must be paid by labor, or, at best, by labor and land."

"But the wiser class of political economists reject the protective system, and defend free trade."

"I do not know whether the free traders or the protectionists are the wiser; I only know that neither can remedy the evil. Free trade simply gives the advantage to those nations that have already got the start of the others in the production of exchangeable commodities. Its maxim is to buy where you can buy cheapest, and to sell where you can sell dearest, and its interest is therefore to enhance as much as possible the profits of capital by diminishing the cost of labor, and therefore the value to the laborer of his labor, the only commodity he has to dispose of. The only difference I can see between the two systems is, that the protective system taxes the land and labor of the nation that adopts it, and the free trade system taxes the land and labor of all trading nations for the benefit of capital, especially of the capital of the nation that has already the start of the others. Free trade is, undoubtedly, the interest of British capital, for Great Britain is the greatest manufacturing and commercial nation of the world; and perhaps for the United States, so largely engaged in the production of agricultural staples and raw materials. Free trade between Great Britain and France, Spain, Germany, Italy, would operate to the advantage of British capital. Besides, trade itself creates a competition for the markets of the world, which originates nearly all the wars of modern times, and necessitates those large standing armies of European states which are such a heavy burden on land and labor."

"But the Reverend Father himself is forgetful; he forgets that commerce is the grand civilizer of nations; that it brings all nations into communion with one another, and binds them together by one and the same interest."

"I am no enemy to commerce, but I should be much obliged to you if you would name to me a single barbarous or semi-barbarous people, in either ancient or modern times, that commerce has civilized."

"The great commercial nations of the world are precisely those which are called civilized nations, which proves that commerce and civilization go together."

"The statement is rather too broad. Ancient Rome was not a commercial nation. France has never been predominantly commercial; nor Germany, either of the north or of the south. But let that pass. That the great commercial nations have been and are civilized nations, and that they have extended the area of civilization by establishing colonies of emigrants from their own bosom, is undoubtedly true; but the point is, has commerce ever civilized a nation it found on opening trade with it uncivilized? I recollect no instance of the kind. As far as my historical reading goes, the only force that has ever civilized a savage, barbarous, or semi-barbarous tribe or people, is religion. Commerce brings civilized and uncivilized nations in contact, no doubt, but as a rule the uncivilized are broken, as the earthen pot that comes in contact with the iron pot. What has the commerce of Great Britain done for India, where civilization was once far superior to what it is now? Great Britain, and perhaps other Christian nations, have gained by it, but India herself has lost her autonomy and been impoverished by it. The people of India are poorer to-day, find it harder to live, than when the English East India Company was formed. England, to obtain a market for her own wares, broke up the native manufactures, and reduced the poor people to abject dependence. The same process has been begun with China and Japan, though it may not be so successful there as it has been in India, where the natives have thus far deteriorated, and in no sense advanced in civilization. Commerce has only one principle—'to buy cheap and sell dear;' it does not concern itself with civilization."

"Then you would annihilate commerce, break up our labor - saving machinery, destroy our steamboats and railroads, and go back to the ox-team, the spinning-wheel, and the hand-loom —back to the Dark Ages. That is the spirit of your religion. Said I not true, then, that your Church opposes progress and resists modern civilization?".

"Not at all. I am not arguing against progress, but simply endeavoring to show that some things so called, may, after all, not deserve that respectable name. I propose no going back to former industrial arrangements. True, I do not believe all is gold that glisters, nor that the people are really any better off under the new system than they were before it was adopted; but since it is adopted, and habits and modes of action are conformed and adjusted to it, we could not dispense with it without causing a far greater evil than was caused by its introduction and adoption. The Church can use your railroads and steamboats for her missionaries, and your lightning telegraphs for rapid communication between her head and members. If it was no advantage to make the change, it still would be a great disadvantage to be forced to return to the past. The Church may, as a question of human prudence, regard certain changes as unadvisable, but if they leave her full freedom of action for herself, and do not conflict with faith, or with what in her discipline is unalterable without serious detriment to its efficiency, she, when they are once effected, accepts them as facts, and adjusts her modes of action to them."

I was not prepared to agree or even disagree

with the priest in his views of the comparative merits of the modern industrial system, or, as Nicholas of Russia called it, "the mercantile system," which was inaugurated by the Peace of Utrecht, in 1713, and at the head of which stands Great Britain; but as he evidently spoke his own views on the subject, not in the name of the Church, I could see nothing in them that committed her against modern civilization. Many facts occurred to me in favor of the priest's views. Under the olden system the people often suffered from famine, occasioned by short crops, by war, and by pestilence, which always follows a dearth of provisions; but I am not aware that when there was plenty in the land, that any one who was able and willing to work must starve, because he could find no work to do. I recalled the fact that so often struck me in my foreign travels, that the greatest distress among the operatives, and the most squalid wretchedness that came under my eye, I invariably found in the leading industrial and commercial nations. Nowhere did I find the extremes of wealth and poverty so striking as in Great Britain. The wealth of her nobility was often great, but that was, in most cases, due to the enhanced value of their landed estates, and led to no painful reflections. But the huge wealth of her merchant princes, her cotton or industrial lords, her bankers and money-changers, contrasted sadly with the mighty mass of pauperism, every day increasing, and supported by rates levied on householders, themselves often but a shade above the pauper. I could not but think, by what a terrible tax on the laboring classes their enormous wealth must have been accumulated. Their wealth has been gained at the expense not only of the laboring class of their own country, but at the expense of the laboring classes of British India, and of all nations against which Great Britain holds the balance of trade. It has been gained by coining the toil, the sweat, the tears, and the blood of millions; and what can I say in defence of the system that permits, encourages, nay, demands for its success, such gross outrages upon our fellow-men?

I see the same system adopted in my own country, whose prosperity, up to the breaking out of the late civil war, was due to three principal causes—the large tracts of fertile land, easily accessible, and cheap; to southern slavery, which stimulated the production of cotton; and the mighty influx into the non-slaveholding States of foreign laborers. To these, and not to our democratic institutions, nor to any wise legislation, state or national, which has from the first been about as unwise, as shortsighted, and as blundering as it well could be, do we owe our prosperity. Slavery is abolished, the public lands are remote from the great centres of population, and the best and richest of them have been given away to great corporations, and the British system, before the war confined mostly to the Northern States, and against which the Confederate States waged their disastrous war, can now spread over the whole Union, and produce, in time, more fatal results than in England, for it meets here no counterpoise in a landed aristocracy, and the government operates simply as its agent or instrument.

We declaim against feudalism, under which the great vassals of the crown were more powerful than the crown itself, and often reduced the central authority to a legal fiction. How much better is it with us, where the effective power is vested in huge railroad and other corporations? The government, both state and national, is only the factor of these corporations, which, though its own creations, it cannot control, but must obey.

These and other considerations make it impossible for me to say the priest was wrong; and yet, a man of the nineteenth century, I hardly dare hint, even to myself, the possibility of his being right. It is true, I have an aversion to trade, and never find any music in the clack of the cotton-mill, but I have not the courage to think that what almost every man I meet boasts as a miracle of progress, can possibly be no progress at all.

CHAPTER IV.

THE conversation was interrupted, as the priest made his last remark on the modern industrial or mercantile system, by an unexpected arrival, at our quiet watering-place, of a fashionable lady, with two marketable—I beg pardon, two marriageable daughters, and was not resumed for several days. The lady had been misinformed, and was much disappointed in not finding our mountain spa a fashionable watering-place. It is true, the guests were all gentlemen, but unhappily, all except the priest and myself were married. The priest was old, and besides was bound, as a priest, to celibacy, and I was, for reasons of my own, no marrying man. The mother was pleasant, amiable, chatty, and the daughters were charming, and we were sorry to have them leave us. But they concluded the waters would not agree with them, and on the morning of the third day after their arrival, they left us for Saratoga. Their departure took from us a ray of sunshine, and cast a sombre hue for a little while over our lonely village, and indisposed us to listen to the grave discussions between the priest and the progressive journalist.

But several days after the departure of our lady guests, the editor and priest resumed their conversations in the usual place. As I drew near, I heard the priest say:

"After all, my dear Journalist, what in modern civilization, that is manifestly a progress, do you pretend the Church opposes and condemns?"

"She condemns the very ideas and principles on which modern civilization is based, such as the dignity and worth of human nature, the perfectibility of the species, the inalienable right of every man to think for himself and to be exempt from all obligation in religion, morals, or politics, to obey, or even to consult any authority but his own reason and judgment, and the doctrine that no one is bound to obey any government but such as claims no powers not derived from the consent of the governed."

"With regard to the dignity and worth of human nature, she probably rates them somewhat higher than you do, for she teaches that God assumed human nature into hypostatic union with himself, and made it his own nature, without its ceasing to be distinctively and properly human nature. With regard to the perfectibility of the species, I will only say that she teaches that man can be regenerated and supernaturalized, and that he is not only perfectible, but by grace can attain to perfection, to the actualization of all the possibilities of his nature. With regard to reason and authority, she requires every man to retain and exercise his reason to the fullest extent, and she demands obedience to no authority that is not reasonable. As to government or power, she teaches with St. Paul and all sound philosophy, that *non est potestas nisi a Deo*, there is no power but from God. Do you not agree with St. Paul?"

"I hold with the American Congress of 1776, and the immortal Jefferson."

"Jefferson was, I doubt not, a sincere and earnest American patriot, a skillful diplomatist, and a very distinguished man; but I hardly think you would be willing to publish in your journal that you hold the author of the Declaration of American Independence to be higher authority than the great Doctor of the Gentiles and author of the Epistle to the Romans. The American Congress of 1776 was, I have always understood, a highly respectable body of men, deserving to be held in high honor by their countrymen. As a naturalized American citizen, I respect their act, but in case they put forth doctrines that conflict with the teachings of St. Paul, I must beg leave to consider the Apostle, who taught by the inspiration of the Holy Ghost, as the higher authority."

"You then differ from the American Congress?"

"I must obey God rather than men, and the authority of the Apostle overrides any and every human authority. The opinions or theories put forth in the Declaration of Independence, form no part of the American Constitution, or of American law, and I can reject them, if I see reason for so doing, without committing any act of disloyalty to the American state. The principles asserted in the preamble to the Declaration, I presume, are to be interpreted by the act they are intended to justify, and I see no right that you or I have to give them a broader sense than the occasion demanded. The Congress were about to declare the Anglo-American colonies they represented absolved from their allegiance to the British crown, and to be free and independent states, and all they needed to affirm was, that every government derives its just powers from the consent of the people who are to be governed, or to live under it, not from the will or might of a foreign nation, prince, or potentate. This I do not deny; for I hold, with the great body of Catholic theologians, that power is under God a trust from the people or nation; but if you understand the Congress to mean that no government has any power to govern any individual except by his personal consent, or that the government derives its just powers from the people in their individual and personal capacity, I must differ widely from it. The law derives its force as law from the lawgiver, and from the people only in the sense in which they make the law, which certainly is not in their personal and individual capacity. The court will hardly permit the murderer to plead that he has never consented to the law under which he is to be tried, or that declares murder a crime, and that he refuses his assent to the penalty it requires to be inflicted on those who commit it. Such a plea, if admitted, would very soon put an end to all courts of criminal jurisdiction, to all government indeed, and leave every man to live as he lists. I cannot, however, believe that the American Congress ever meant anything so anti-social and absurd. As I understand it, there is no conflict between it and St. Paul."

"I want no better proof than this, that the Church opposes the essential principle of modern civilization. She denies, as you virtually concede, that government derives all its just powers from the governed, and therefore asserts its right to govern me without my consent. She therefore denies the sovereignty of the people."

"The sovereignty of the individual, or of the people as individuals, most certainly; of the people collectively understood, or the people as the community, by no means. In this latter sense, the sovereignty of the people, the political people, is nothing peculiar to modern civilization, but has always been asserted by all civilized nations, and is, as we have seen, the distinctive principle of civilization itself; the former, which is, in principle, only a phase of despotism, has never been asserted or submitted to by any civilized people on earth. That there is in most modern states a party more or less numerous that plead it in justification of their conspiracies, insurrections, rebellions, or revolutionary movements against legally existing governments, I do not deny; but this doctrine forms the basis of no modern state, and even these, when they attain to power, are forced to abandon it. You mistake as the actual basis of modern civilization, the principle which a party is everywhere struggling to make its basis, but which is as yet not so made."

"The state with us is confessedly founded on these principles—on the sacred right of insurrection, rebellion, revolution."

"I think not; I find no such right recognized or provided for in the Constitution. I find treason recognized as a high crime, and generally punishable with death. That even the American people do not practically hold the principles you allege, is evident from their recent war in vindication of the Union against armed secession. Whether the secession of States is rebellion or not, depends on the fact whether American sovereignty vests in the States severally, or in the States united. If the former be the fact, secession is no rebellion, is only the exercise, saving the breach of faith, of a right inherent in each of the several States, and never surrendered to the Union; if in the States united, the Confederates, in making war on the Union, were rebels. In which vests the sovereignty I am not the authority to decide. The Church gave her Sacraments to men on either side alike; but the American people, as represented by the government, called secession rebellion, and put it down by armed force, and thus proved that they are very far from conceding, in any practical sense, that government can rightfully exercise no power not derived from the consent of the governed. On the principle you contend for, not only States but individuals may secede or withdraw themselves from the government whenever they please, or find it convenient. If your interpretation of the Declaration of Independence is the true one, the war against secession was wholly indefensible. But I am aware of no government that does not assert its right of self-preservation against any and every class of assailants, whether from within or from without."

"I do not deny the right of self-defence to the government, or its right to put down rebellion, or suppress revolt."

"Therefore, you concede the authority of the nation, and deny that of the individual citizen, or of any combination of individual citizens, to rebel against it or to resist it, and abandon, very properly, the principle that government has no just powers not derived from the personal consent of the individuals governed; for it cannot be pretended that they who resist or rebel against the government consent to it."

"Modern civilization is not so much the civilization that actually obtains, as that to which the modern world is tending, or that is struggling to be the civilization of the future. There is much of the leaven of the past still retained in the present, which must be cast out, before it can become actual."

"It is no insignificant fact that the party which wars against the Church is always the party of the future, and never attains, but is always just a-going to attain to the good it seeks. Your modern civilization is something that is just a-going to be effected."

"That is because men and society are infinitely progressive. They pursue and struggle to realize an ideal that is always just above and before them, and which recedes as they advance. No individual ever overtakes his ideal. The individual is finite, the ideal is infinite. The greatness, the glory of man, is not that he is perfect, but that he is infinitely perfectible; is always nearing perfection, but never reaching it—in the fact that there are no limits to his progress. His happiness is not in the quarry, but in the chase."

"I am parched with thirst; I see the waters of the cool, bubbling spring; I run towards it; it recedes; and the faster, the faster I run. I am faint with hunger; before me is a table spread with rich viands and precious fruits; I hasten towards it, it recedes as I advance, and keeps always in sight, but just beyond my reach, and never a morsel can I obtain. This is the happiness you promise me, the glory of my nature, of which you speak, and the advanced civilization you condemn the Church for not approving! Why, my dear friend, you offer me as heaven what the Greeks imagined to be hell, and proffer me as bliss what they thought was the severest punishment to which armipotent and triumphant Jove could doom the defeated giant Tantalus."

"You seem to forget, Reverend Father, that a poet of your own Church, if I mistake not, has sung:

> 'Hope springs eternal in the human breast,
> Man never is, but always to be blest'"

"No, I forget not; but I need something more than rhyme, whether I am to take it gravely or satirically, to persuade me that it is happiness never to be happy, a blessing never to be blest, to hunger and thirst and never be filled. A greater than the poet Pope said, 'Blessed are ye that hunger and thirst after justice, for ye *shall be satisfied.*' Hope is a great consoler, but I do not understand how there can be hope where there is full assurance that fruition is impossible. There would be despair, not hope. Sweet is repose after labor, and the hope of obtaining it makes the labor light. But when you tell me the labor will be eternally in vain, that the hour of repose will never come, that there remaineth no rest after toil, no calm after the storm, no peace after the war, you deprive me of heart and hope, and make life a weary burden, too heavy to be borne."

"But the labor is not in vain. It is in the labor, in the chase, in the effort, in the struggle, in the battle that the powers of the mind, and soul, and body are developed and strengthened."

"To what end? What avail the development, the strengthening, the growth of our faculties, when there is no maturity for them, no end to be gained? It is only the hope of winning that stimulates us to labor, and sustains us under our fatigue. Your doctrine deprives us of hope, by teaching us that it is an illusion. That your doctrine of progress is false, you might infer from the very fact that to effect it an illusion is necessary. Take away the illusion of hope, and you render every effort impossible. Can that be true which is possible only by an illusion, a falsehood?"

It seemed to me that here the priest had the better of the editor. I had early been divested of all my illusions; I no longer saw anything to gain, and had ceased to make any effort; my mind and affections became stagnant, and I vegetated under an intolerable lassitude and weariness of life rather than lived. I had adopted, without much reflection, the modern doctrine of perfectibility, or indefinite progress. While its novelty lasted, and the illusions of youth were undissipated by experience, I was active, and exerted my faculties in various directions. I found pleasure in activity; in the effort, in the chase, and said the happiness is in striving to attain, not in the attainment. Possession dispels the illusion; nothing turns out to be what we expected; we turn away wearied and disgusted from the possession of that which we had moved heaven and earth to gain. But when the illusion is once dispelled by experience, and we see no object of pursuit large enough to fill the soul, to satisfy all its wants, and afford it ever fresh delight, we cease to exert ourselves. I became apathetic, took no interest in anything, looked upon all the pursuits, pleasures, pains, hopes, and fears of my fellow-men, with listless indifference. One thing was as good as another; all was vanity. *Vanitas vanitatum, et omnia vanitas.* My life had no object, no aim, no purpose, and I thought only of how to tide over the present hour.

The priest startled me by showing me that those who placed, as I had done, the good in always pursuing an ideal, and never attaining it, simply mistake hell for heaven. All the torture, the agony of soul, all the tragedy of life, comes from unrealized ideals. The age in which we live, perhaps more than any other, is in pursuit of ideals never to be realized. Hence its restlessness, its agitation, its frivolity, its feebleness, its abasement of character, its ill-at-ease, its craving for stimulants of all sorts, for body, mind, and soul. O, if one could only fully believe him who says, "Come unto me all ye that labor and are heavy laden, and I will give you rest;" "Blessed are ye who hunger and thirst after righteousness, for ye shall be filled;" "'Blessed are ye that mourn, for ye shall be comforted." O, is it true that there remaineth a rest for the soul!

CHAPTER V.

THE priest replied, "You are right, my dear Editor, in saying man is progressive, and in holding that the ideal which floats above and before him, and draws him upward and onward, is infinite. It is infinite; and we are finite. However near to it we may advance, or however near to us it may be, it is always infinitely above and beyond us. You touch here, without knowing it, the great mystery of human life, and which is inexplicable to all men who have hope only in this world, and see nothing beyond the grave. Have you ever asked yourself what that ideal is? Is it real? Is it a vain illusion? Is it a creation of your own fancy? Is it yóur own mind projected? or, is it the real end for which you are created, to which the soul so nobly aspires, and without union with which she can neither attain the complement of her nature, or the beatitude she craves?"

"Your question is metaphysical, and I eschew metaphysics. The moment a man enters into the field of metaphysics, he loses himself in a dense fog, in which he can neither see nor be seen. I make it a rule to give the metaphysicians and theologians a wide berth. I am contented with practical common sense, and deal only with realities. I am of Anglo-Saxon descent."

"Your Anglo-Saxon ancestors are doubtless proud of their gifted descendant. But the man who professes to regard it as a merit to eschew philosophy and theology, should studiously avoid raising questions which, in the nature of the case, only philosophy and theology can answer. You have all along been engaged in philosophy and theology, though it may be without being aware of it. You tell us there hovers ever before us an infinite ideal, which we are always striving to realize, but which forever eludes us. I think even Anglo-Saxon common sense can comprehend that this ideal is either something or nothing, and that, since it moves and agitates us, it can hardly be nothing. The same common sense, I think, must suffice to assure us that if it is infinite and we finite, it is something distinct from and independent of us, and not ourselves projected. The finite projected can be only finite. It is, then, no more than a dictate of common sense, to conclude that the infinite ideal you assert is and can be only real and infinite being, that is, what philosophers and theologians call God, and that in her endless craving for the ideal, the soul has what old Cudworth would call a *prolepsis* of her end in God. Do you concede it?"

"I discuss no such questions, and therefore neither affirm nor deny anything of the matter?"

"Well, respecting your ignorance, since you honestly avow it, permit me to say that a man's ideal must always be greater than he actually is, or otherwise it would be no ideal at all. An infinite ideal must be God, for he alone is infinite, and in him the ideal and the real, or the actual and the possible, are identical. The idea must be infinite, or man could not be infinitely progressive as you say he is. The soul in craving and seeking to possess the ideal, in which you place progress, craves and seeks to possess God in a sense that she does not as yet possess him. She now possesses God, lives and moves, and has her being in him as her Creator. The ideal is before us, not behind us; something to be approached, not recoiled from. The ideal is the end we are striving to realize, but which, you say, can never be realized or attained to. But the infinite ideal is God: God revealing himself, not as our Maker, but as our End, our final cause, to whom we return, and in whom our progress finds its term. Say, then, not that we are infinitely progressive, but that we are progressive to the infinite, and that the soul cannot rest till it attains to the infinite God. Progress is not indefinite, then, but has a term, and that term is the infinite God, not, as you assume, an abstraction; and the infinite God is our final cause, as he is our first cause. When we have reached our end, we have attained, have found, possess our beatitude, and our progress terminates: for we have reached the infinite, and I think even you will concede that there is no advance beyond the infinite, and that the infinite is large enough to fill and satisfy the most hungry soul."

"But how do you prove that the infinite God is the term of our progress?"

"You eschew metaphysics, so I can only answer, that you assert that man is infinitely progressive; but this can only mean that he is progressive even to the infinite, to oneness with the infinite God, for we have before settled it that progress is motion forward, an advance towards an end? Without a term to be reached, a goal to be attained, or at least to be aimed at, progress would be inconceivable, and there could be no forward or backward motion. Do not forget the illustration of the treadmill, or, if you please, that of a man trying to step on his own shadow. Remember that you cannot assert progress without asserting for it both a starting-point and a terminating point—a beginning and an end— therefore, my son, *aspice finem*, look to the end, which, through Christ the Mediator is, I dare assert, attainable, if you will, realizable."

"Grant the ideal is God, that God can fill the soul, yet we may never attain to him or realize our ideal: we may miss the realization."

"That is well said; for men are free agents, and it is to be feared that many do miss their end, fail to fulfil their destiny, by preferring the creature to the Creator, a finite to an infinite good, and by refusing to concur with the grace and to use the means necessary to gain it. These are, in the language of Christians, lost; are doomed to hell or the lower regions; but they are as lost in precisely the condition which you assume is the normal condition of all men, that of pursuing forever an ideal which they can never realize or attain to; of seeking and never finding; doomed to hunger and thirst without ever being filled; to crave what they have not, and to see it always elude them, and to be deprived of all hope of ever attaining. They are in what you call heaven, but in what Christians call hell; they are, according to you, manifesting the greatness, the dignity, and the glory of human nature; but to the Christian they are 'clouds without water, which are carried about by the winds; trees of the autumn, unfruitful, twice dead, plucked up by the roots; raging waves of the sea, foaming out their own confusion; wandering stars to whom the storm of darkness [despair] is reserved forever,' as St. Jude describes them. They have failed of their destiny, and remain always below it, with the Infinite Ideal, henceforth for them, forever unrealizable, floating above and beyond their reach."

"You paint nothing, Reverend Father, to frighten me, and the condition you describe is, as far as I can see, no less bearable than our present condition, which I find so pleasant that I am loth to leave it."

"So I expected a true son of the nineteenth century to answer. But here you are sustained by hope; there all hope is left behind, and only black despair goes with you. Yet, let me tell you, my young friend, that when you have lived to my age, and gone through what I have, you will not find your present pleasure in the effort, the struggle, the pursuit; you will be glad to find that the battle is one day to be over, that the victory is to be won, and that henceforth you may throw off your harness, for there is laid up for you a crown of life that fadeth not away, eternal in the heavens."

There was no sadness in the priest's tones; his face wore a smile of victory, and it was evident that he was looking forward, with joy unspeakable, to the hour when he should be released and welcomed to the eternal home where was his love. I looked at him as he ceased speaking, and asked myself is it possible that faith is something more than opinion, and Christianity something more than a theorem for philosophers? Here the conversation ended for the day, and I sought solitude, that I might reflect on the great questions which it had raised in my mind in spite of myself.

The metropolitan editor evidently was proof against anything the priest could say, and if, for a moment he seemed, like King Agrippa, to be almost persuaded on some points, he soon verified the old maxim—

> "A man persuaded against his will,
> Is of the same opinion still."

He amused himself, and whiled away the time by calling out the priest, whom he admired not for his deep earnestness, sincerity, and evident good faith, but as a skillful lawyer speaking from his brief. He himself probably had no very deep convictions of any sort. Like too many of his fraternity, he had never seriously thought for himself on any subject once in his life; he had simply inquired for the dominant opinion or tendency of his age, his country, his party, or his coterie, and supported it without raising the question whether it was right or wrong. He called it the will of the people, the voice of the people; and the voice of the people, you know, is the voice of God. He had taken up with the modern doctrine of progress, sneered at everything old, and lauded everything new. The priest, as an old man, who had seen many revolutions in states and empires, and had reflected much on what he had seen, was inclined to believe that all wisdom and virtue was not born with the nineteenth century, that "brave men lived before Agamemnon," and that the birth of the Saviour was a greater event for the human race than the French Revolution of 1789.

CHAPTER VI.

THE next day the priest did not make his appearance. It was, as I afterwards learned, the anniversary of a sad event in his memory, when several' of his near relatives and dear friends were massacred while endeavoring to protect their church and its altar from desecration by a band of revolutionists. The editor spent the day with one or two of his friends in rambling over the green hills and climbing the mountains in pursuit of the picturesque; the rest of us congregated at the usual place, under the huge old maples and beeches, and conversed among ourselves on the ideas advanced by the priest. The general sympathy, as a matter of course, was with the editor, only most of the guests thought he pushed his views of progress a little too far, and that in some of his notions he was too transcendental; but all dissented *in toto*, except perhaps myself, from the priest's political economy. His doctrine, if true, would strip the present century of its special glory. What! intimate that the present industrial system operates to break up small home industries, and to make the rich richer, and the poor poorer! It was downright treason, nay, blasphemy, for it blasphemed the works of genius, and genius is divine.

The day after, the editor resumed the discussion with the priest, though on a different point.

"You and your Church, Reverend Father, make too little of the progress of liberty in your estimate of modern civilization. Civil liberty has made and is making immense progress."

"In imperial France, imperial Austria, autocratic Russia, despotic Prussia, aristocratic England, oppressed Ireland, newfangled Italy, revolutionary Spain, and anarchical Spanish America?"

"In the United States we have a republic based on the principle of the equality of all men without regard to race or complexion."

"A principle proclaimed more than eighteen centuries ago, by the Church of God, embodied in the Civil Law, and always acted on and realized in the Church herself, or the Commonwealth of Christ. The Church has never known any distinction of race or complexion, and she has always had the same service for the master and the servant, and the same law and the same discipline for the prince and the peasant. The

United States, I hope I may say without offence, are not the whole world, and their political principles are practically adopted by no other nation. I own you are a great people, but you have at best only applied, in the political order, the principles the Church has always taught and insisted on. If I am not misinformed, it is even yet doubtful if the no-distinction policy between the white race and the colored races—black, red and yellow—will be sustained by a majority of the American people. You are in the midst of a struggle, the result of which is, as yet, uncertain. It is not many years since you held, in round numbers, four millions of people out of thirty-one millions, in slavery, and treated them as chattels. It is too soon to boast of your progress in liberty."

"But Russia has emancipated her serfs."

"Very true: at least what is called emancipating them; but, as I read history, there were no serfs in Russia till near the beginning of the sixteenth century. The autocracy, due to the usurper, Peter the Great, remains, and the progress effected is, at best, only a partial return to the liberty enjoyed in Russia prior to the date of what you call modern civilization."

"Count you for nothing the fact that both

Prussia and Austria have become constitutional states, with parliamentary governments?"

"It is only to-day that they have become so. As yet the Prussian constitution is only a paper constitution, and practically the government is a military despotism, as much so as under Frederic the Second. The Austrian constitution has hardly as yet got into working order, and I have not been able to discover in it any guaranty for any greater liberty to the people than they had previously enjoyed. Von Beust governs as absolutely as did Prince Kaunitz, with whom Austria's misfortunes began. You count, I presume, the extinction of the once great and free kingdom of Poland by Prussia, Russia, and Austria as a progress of freedom. The rights and independence of nations do not seem to have any connection in the modern political mind with liberty."

"Italy, long divided into petty states, held in tutelage by despotic Austria and the no less despotic Pope, and reduced to a mere geographical expression, has been, with the exception of the city of Rome and its adjacent territory, emancipated politically from the despotism of both, and united into a single state under a liberal monarchy and a popular constitution. She now belongs to herself, and is one of the Great Powers of Europe. Is that nothing?"

"The events that have occurred in the Italian peninsula are of too recent a date to afford you any solid argument. What is to be the future of the Italian peninsula, I do not pretend to foretell; your so-called kingdom of Italy is in the process of formation rather than definitively formed, and Italian statesmen are attempting to found it in iniquity, by the violation of international law, or the disregard of vested rights, and the suppression of the freedom and independence of sovereign states. I have no faith in paper or parchment constitutions, or constitutions which are drawn up with 'malice aforethought,' and which have no support in the habits and traditions of the people who are to live under them. Such constitutions can be upheld only by military force, and no government upheld only by military force, with no moral hold on the people, is likely to work well, or to stand a long time. Italy, for more reasons than one, is very dear to me, and I cannot wish her ill; but as yet the Italian people are practically less free, and far more heavily taxed, than they were under their legitimate princes, who have been so violently and iniquitously dispossessed."

"But while we are talking, news comes of a revolution in Spain and the expulsion of Isabella Segunda, and a free republic or a constitutional monarchy will be established by the free action of the Spanish people. Surely that is a progress of liberty."

"I know not that. There is a strong republican party in the large Spanish towns, but the great majority of the population of the country are attached to monarchy, and if left free will vote for a king. The government overthrown was a parliamentary government, a constitutional monarchy. Spain is my native country, and the news distresses me. I never acknowledged Isabella for my sovereign, for she had by Spanish law no right to the Spanish throne; but I credit none of the rumors against her character as a woman or as a queen. She has fallen a victim to the revolutionary spirit of the day, not because she was immoral, tyrannical, or capricious, but because she loved the Church and sympathized with the Holy Father in his manifold troubles, and perhaps because a brother-in-law wanted her crown. Spain was once a free state, the freest in Europe, till she fell under Austrian sovereigns, who destroyed her communeros, and reduced her nobles to mere courtiers.

Each of her provinces and towns had its fueros, its rights and privileges, which even her Austrian and Bourbon kings respected, but which revolutions professedly in favor of popular freedom have swept away. For the last few years, under the government of Isabella and the Cortes, she has been rapidly recovering from the abyss into which thirty years of revolution and disorder had plunged her; her trade and industry have been reviving, internal improvements encouraged, religion—as far as the queen's power extended—fostered, and the day seemed not distant when she would proudly resume in the European congress of nations her place as a Great-Power. What is in store for her in the future, I know not; I fear it is only anarchy, civil war, and a baser prostration. Cite her not, I pray you, as a proof of the progress of liberty, if you wish me to believe the liberty you talk of is a thing the Church should bless, or from which civilization has anything to hope. Do not force me to exclaim with Madame Roland, on her way to the scaffold, to which the revolution she had done so much to foment and to urge on in its devastating career, conducted her, 'O liberty, what crimes are committed in thy name!' Yes, Dame Roland, you felt it, when your turn came to reap the fruit of your own sowing."

"But little as you think, Reverend Father, of the liberty gained by the people of Europe in this brave and generous struggle against the despotisms of kings and nobles, you cannot deny that they have emancipated themselves from the despotism of the Pope, and broken the galling chains of the old union of Church and State."

"The old union of Church and State is dissolved, and no government now on earth, unless fallen Portugal be an exception, acknowledges its obligation of spiritual obedience to the Vicar of Christ, the supreme pastor, teacher, and governor of the Universal Church; but whether that is a gain or a loss to liberty, to the state, or to the people, is another matter. The Pope never claimed any temporal authority out of the States of the Church, though he exercised for a time an arbitratorship of Christian nations, poorly replaced by your modern congresses and conferences of sovereigns; but that was an accident, and no essential element of the papacy. The nations, not the papacy, have suffered by the change. In all other respects the authority of the Pope was spiritual, and the emancipation of the nations you boast is simply emancipation from the law of God, and the assertion of the independence of the secular order, or its freedom to dispense with justice and morality in politics. I have yet to learn that the people have gained anything by this sort of emancipation. Kings and princes have gained the power of violating all laws, human and divine, without exposing themselves to the spiritual discipline of the Church. That is all that has been gained, as far as I can see. You are obliged to resort to revolution and bloody and disastrous civil war to effect now what once could generally be effected peaceably by a brief from the acknowledged spiritual head of Christendom. Even from your purely human point of view this seems to me more like a loss than a gain."

"I see the old spirit survives, and that those who oppose the spread of the Church here on the ground of her incompatibility with the existence of our free institutions, and the sovereignty of the people, are right. You regret the lost union of Church and State, and if you had the power you would re-establish it here."

"That by no means follows: I may regret the passing away of things which I believe were in their day good and useful, and yet be very unwilling to restore them. The relation of the Church to the state, which subsisted in the Middle Ages, I believe was a proper relation at that time, and served the interests both of religion and of society; but times have changed, and that relation is no longer practicable nor even desirable. Whether the changes that have taken place are for the better or for the worse, it is useless to inquire. They have taken place, and the Church in fulfilling her divine mission takes the world where she finds it. She did not treat the feudal *régime* as she had treated the Roman imperial *régime*, nor will she treat the republican society of America as she did the feudal society of Europe, or the monarchical society that supplanted the feudal. She will assert here, as always and everywhere, the supremacy of the law of God, for states as for individuals, and the incompetency of the state in spirituals. Here and elsewhere, all she asks is protection in her free and independent performance of her own work, or in her freedom and independence in governing in spiritual matters her own children according to her own law. She can have no motive or disposition to change the constitution of your republic, for under it she has nearly all she ever struggled with the civil authorities of the Old World to obtain. The only thing she has any motive to strive for here is to prevent any fundamental change in the constitution and laws in regard to the relations of Church and state."

"That sounds plausible enough, and is the proper thing for you to say here. Yet you know perfectly well, Reverend Father, that the Church condemns those of her children who advocate the separation of Church and State."

"Those she condemns are not those who mean by the separation of Church and state the order established by the Constitution of the American Republic, but those who mean by it the absolute independence and supremacy of the secular order, the emancipation of the state from the law of God, its freedom to suppress the Church whenever it finds her in the way of its ambition, its policy, its schemes of injustice against either its own subjects or against foreign states. In the Old World the separation of Church and state means the supremacy of the state alike in spirituals and temporals, as in Russia, Prussia, Great Britain, and other states, or at least, the right of the state to define the boundaries of the Church, and to enlarge or contract the sphere of her freedom at will. This right is claimed, is asserted for itself in every European state, and the state holds itself free to restrict the freedom of the Church or to exclude her altogether, as it sees proper. This claim renders concordats or treaties between the Church and the State necessary in order to secure to the Church some degree of freedom and independence. What the Church condemns under the head of separation of Church and State, is the independence of the state of the laws of God, the abrogation of these concordats, and the right of the state to abrogate them by its own authority without her consent, as has been done in the Italian states by the pretended kingdom of Italy, and more recently by Austria, which places the Church at the mercy of the state. In your republic concordats are not necessary. The state disclaims all authority in spirituals, and by its fundamental law recognizes the independence and freedom of the spiritual order, and its obligation to protect and defend the Church with all its power in the peaceable exercise of her spiritual freedom, which is more than the most favorable concordat has ever yet secured to her elsewhere. There is no country in the world where the Church is or ever has been as free to govern her children according to her own discipline and laws, or where Pius IX. is so truly Pope as the United States. And this freedom is not held here as a grant from the state revocable at its will, but is the right of conscience of each and every citizen; one of those rights of man, or rather of God, which are antecedent to civil society, and which government is instituted to protect and defend. Rome would have but a small share of that wisdom and sagacity she gets credit for, if she should seek or suffer her children to seek to substitute for this system any system which does or ever has obtained in the Old World."

"But this freedom which the Church has here she has only in common with all religious denominations. With that she never has been and never will be satisfied. She would reign alone; and when she gets the power she will compel the state to suppress all religious denominations hostile to herself. Such is at least a fair inference from her past history."

"I think not. She has never had in the past a state of things such as obtains here, and therefore no inference of the kind can be drawn from her past history. The Church is exclusive, intolerant, as is truth itself, in the theological order, but she is obliged by no doctrine or principle she holds, to exact from the state civil intolerance. She does not believe it a matter of indifference in regard to eternal salvation, or even in regard to civil society, whether a man believes truth or error; but she can very well consent, where she is free herself, where all her own rights are protected, and she stands on a footing of civil equality with the sects, that they should be before the state as free as herself. If the state gives them no advantage over her, she can get along very well without its giving her any advantage over them."

Here I confess the priest surprised me. Like the majority of my countrymen, I had supposed the Church is innately and necessarily antagonistic to our republican institutions, and that it would be impossible for her to coexist with them. Naturally tolerant in consequence of a native want of earnestness, and having no very strong religious convictions of my own, I had been willing to allow her an "open field and fair play;" for here she was feeble, and I felt confident that the influence of American intelligence and American freedom would be amply sufficient to prevent her from ever becoming strong enough to be at all dangerous to the American state or to civil and religious liberty. To hear the priest assert that the Church found here all or nearly all she wanted, or *had ever struggled for*, seemed a ridiculous paradox. Was it, indeed, true that the popes in their long and bitter struggle with the German Emperor and other sovereigns had been contending only for that freedom and independence which the state with us recognizes in every religious denomination, and protects as the birthright of every American citizen, and not for supreme power in the state, and the subjugation of the entire secular order to the domination of a haughty and arrogant priesthood?

This was too much. Could Luther and Calvin, Henry and Cranmer, and the great and learned divines of the Anglican and other communions, who for three hundred years have strenuously mantained the contrary, have been deceived or trying to deceive others? Yet here was a priest who seemed to understand himself, who appeared also to be perfectly familiar with the principles and history of his Church, and who was certainly no trimmer, and no courtier of king or people, quietly, and as a matter of course, placing wholly in the wrong those great divines, and nearly the whole Protestant world, who had excused the civil intolerance of the early Reformers and the princes who espoused their cause, on the ground that they only followed the teaching and example of Rome, and asserting, as if it were an admitted truth, that the Church finds here in this land of religious liberty, all or nearly all that she wants, or has ever struggled to gain, and therefore must be led by her own principles and interests to use all her influence, even if gaining the ascendency, to preserve our free institutions, and especially the equal civil and religious rights of all men before the state, which our government is bound by its very constitution to recognize, protect, and defend! It disconcerted all my preconceived notions, set aside what I had supposed to be the final judgment of the world, and denied what I had supposed no one would or could question. I was puzzled. But the able editor was not puzzled or surprised at all, and I listened attentively for his reply.

CHAPTER VII.

"ALL that, Reverend Father, is easily said, and it is decidedly for your interest to say it. Your Church has nearly run itself out in the Old World, and the only remaining hope of the papacy is in gaining the people of the United States; and you well know that were you to tell them the truth, and disclose to them the hopes and designs of Rome, you could not get them to listen to you a moment. Were you to tell them that there is an innate incompatibility between your Church and their republic, they would soon put an end to your mission. You are shrewd enough to understand that your success depends on your persuading them that your Church, instead of opposing, approves the principles of American republicanism, and is necessary for their preservation and free and orderly working. Tell that to the marines; I believe you not; you are no disinterested witness."

"Are you a disinterested witness, my dear Editor?"

"What can you mean by asking me such a question? I have no prejudices, no interest in opposing your Church."

"Let no man say he has no prejudices. You have your pride of opinion to maintain, and are not a man predisposed to yield it up to any one, or to any argument. Interest? You have no more interest, I grant, in opposing the Church than the shrine-makers of Ephesus had in opposing St. Paul. You are simply a shrine-maker, and your idol is public opinion, or at least the public opinion of your party, of which you are also one of the chief priests. You are a leading journalist, and journalism is a power in the American state; but you would be nobody were you to avow yourself a member of the Church, and use your journal to defend her against the misrepresentations and slanders daily inculcated against her, as strenuously as you would if they were attacks on the purity and honor of your mother. You have not as yet the grace nor the earnestness of character for that. You are too well satisfied with yourself as you are, and with the position you hold."

"And what else is to be said of the Reverend Father? What sacrifices has he made?"

"None that I count, though it may be some

sacrifices which you and your countrymen would shrink from; for of all the people I have ever known, democrats as you are, you are the greatest idolators of wealth, rank, and title. I have made no sacrifice, for I count all things as dung and dross, if I can but win Christ, and I have already been rewarded a hundred fold for all I ever gave up for Him. I want no higher glory on earth than to be a priest of the living God, and no greater consolation than to toil and suffer for the salvation of souls. But you are in no disposition to appreciate things of this sort. There is a life that is hidden from you with God, and a joy you have no relish for."

"I certainly am no enthusiast, no fanatic, and I did not suppose you to be either one or the other. I have generally regarded the clergy of your Church as cool, shrewd, calculating, ambitious men, bent on acquiring power for their Church, and unscrupulous as to the means they adopt; devoted to their Church in aiding her to dominate over kings and emperors, over the lives and fortunes, the minds and consciences of men, and to be as supreme on earth as God is in heaven; but I have held them generally as devoid of faith, of conscience, of enthusiasm, fanaticism, as of honor, and ready at all times to act on the maxim, 'The end sanctifies the means.'"

"We sometimes commit a grave mistake, my dear Mr. Editor, when we judge others by ourselves, and transfer our own views, feelings, and aims to persons who live and move in an atmosphere very different from our own, and act from motives which we have no conception of. The life of a simple, sincere, earnest child of the Church is something of which you have had no experience, my friend, and that lies beyond the range of your philosophy. For my part, I do not believe what you think of us is generally true even of the ministers of the Reformed religion. It is difficult for me to conceive the existence of a class of men moved by a spirit so satanic as we must be, if you are right. I can not see in the domination you say we seek to secure for our Church a sufficient motive for our conduct, for really, if we are as shrewd and as good calculators as you pretend, we must see that we do and can gain nothing. I can understand Satan. He sets himself up as the rival of God, seeks to defeat his kingdom, and to get himself worshiped as God. He has a personal end, a personal defeat to avenge, a personal victory to win, a personal malice to gratify. He hates all good, and wars against it wherever he sees it, for he has said to himself, 'Evil, be thou my good; hell, be thou my heaven.' I can understand why he should seek to destroy the kingdom of God, as I can understand why your ministers, deceived by his wiles and carried away by his delusions, should seek to destroy the Church that everywhere confronts and embarrasses them; but my knowledge of human nature does not enable me to conceive how men who believe not the Church to be a divine institution, who credit not her promises or her doctrines, and seek only power over men in this world, could devote their lives, traverse oceans and huge forests, in hunger and fatigue, in toil and infirmity, foregoing all the comforts of civilization, bearing contumely and contempt and persecution even unto death, to build up a powerful corporation, in whose domination they have no personal interest and can have no personal share."

"But do you not consider it a higher honor to be a simple priest of the Church than to be a grandee of Spain or any other nation, than to be even king or kaiser?"

"Unquestionably, but only because I believe the Church to be really the kingdom of God on earth, her doctrines to be the revealed word of God, and her sacraments to be really instituted by Christ himself, and that they really confer the grace they signify, are the channels through which the Holy Ghost is really infused into our hearts, regenerates us, elevates us to a higher life, and makes us heirs and joint-heirs with Christ of eternal glory in the heavens. Take away that belief, suppose me to act from calculation, not faith, from the mere love of earthly power, I should see no glory or greatness in the priesthood, I should find nothing in it to sustain me in my labors, or to console me in my privations, and should say with St. Paul, 'if in this life only we have hope, we are of all men the most miserable.' What could we, if we believed not, see in the domination of the Church, even if we should secure it, worth living for and dying for?"

"You pretend, Reverend Father, that your Church is satisfied with the order established here, and that she really favors the great principles of natural freedom and equality on which our republic is founded. If she approves these principles, and is satisfied with the relations which subsist here between Church and State, why has she nowhere founded the state on the basis of equal rights?"

"The Church is not the state nor the framer of its constitution, and she has not and never has pretended to have temporal authority in the temporal order. She is a spiritual kingdom—the kingdom of God on earth—and she leaves to the civil and political order that which God himself leaves to it—human free will. She has always asserted the great principles which the American people more successfully than any other have carried out in their political constitution, but it has never been her mission to apply them practically out of her own order. Our Lord did not come as a temporal Messiah. The efforts to defend these principles, even in their spiritual application, has raised an almost universal clamor against her for encroaching on the province of the civil power, and are the basis of the principal charges her enemies even now allege against her. What then would have been the outcry, had she attempted to organize political society in accordance with these principles! The relation between Church and State here, which so well meets her wants, can subsist only where the state is founded on the recognition of the freedom of conscience, and the equal rights of all, which it is bound to protect and defend. Never in the Old World has it been humanly possible to found the state on the American doctrine of equal rights embodied in the American Constitution. Neither the Government nor the Church, even if in the province of the Church, could have done it."

"Why not?"

"You, a journalist whose profession it is to instruct the people in their political rights and duties, and who ought therefore to be a master of political science and of true statemanship, ask me such a question? Constitutions of states are not things that can be made to order, and imposed by authority, regardless of the habits, manners, customs, and traditions of the people who are to live under them. England, monarchical and aristocratic to the core, could not get on as a commonwealth, and when the dictator Cromwell died, and left no successor, she recalled the Stuarts, re-established the throne, and restored her old constitution. France, after the example of England, made a revolution, beheaded her king, abolished royalty, abolished nobility, adopted as her motto, 'liberty, equality, and fraternity,' imposed on herself with much ceremony, fanfaronade, beating of drums, and sounding of trumpets, an entire new constitution, made after the most approved pattern; and not only one, but many new constitutions; yet, as Thomas Carlyle says, 'they wouldn't go,' though drawn up by one who boasted that 'politics is a science he had finished.' After a period of military despotism under Napoleon I., she was forced to recall her legitimate king, to reconstruct the throne she had demolished, and reconsecrate the altars she had profaned; and she is even now governed chiefly by military force. Mexico and the South American colonies of Spain asserted their independence of the mother country, adopted constitutions framed after the great Anglo-American model, and have been in a state of anarchy ever since.

"No, sir; constitutions," continued the priest, "cannot be made and imposed on a nation. Lord John Russell's numerous experiments, under the most favorable circumstances, have proved that much. They must be born and developed with the nation; generated, not made, as Count de Maister has amply proved. You may change a dynasty, or the magistracy of a nation, without destroying it, and sometimes with happy results; the constitution of a nation, never. Every true statesman knows this, and seeks always to administer the affairs of the state in accordance with its fundamental constitution. He accepts that constitution as his starting-point and his inflexible law, and labors only to correct abuses that may creep in, to clear away anomalies that the vicissitudes of time or the course of events may create, and to do the best he can with it for the nation. The Church cannot do otherwise, however overwhelming may be her influence. The necessary conditions of such a constitution as that of the United States, have never been found in European society, and do not exist there even yet. Its principles may have been recognized and defended by both statesmen and churchmen, but it has never been possible to organize any European state in accordance with them.

"The peculiarity of the American Constitution," the priest went on, "under the point of view we are now considering it, is not merely in asserting the equality of all men before the law, but in asserting their equal rights as held not from the law, but from the Creator, anterior to civil society, and therefore rights which government is bound by its very constitution to recognize and protect to the full extent of its power. This view of rights you will not find in the Greek and Roman republics. Under them man was held to exist for the state, and had no rights but such as he held from it. You will not find it in the

Roman Empire, which differed from the republic only in that it aggregated the several functions of the state to the emperor. Under feudalism you had the Roman imperial system, and in addition not the rights of man, but the personal rights of the feudal chief. All your boasted progress in Europe consists in eliminating, sometimes peaceably, sometimes violently, the feudal element, and in rendering exclusive Roman imperialism on the one hand, or the pagan republic on the other, as Mazzini and Garibaldi are seeking to do in Italy, the Radicals in England, and the Progresistas in Spain. Is your question answered?"

"You have not, Reverend Father, proved to my satisfaction, that the Church, if she gains the ascendency, will not require the state to use its power to suppress all sects opposed to her, and forbid the profession of any creed or dogma contrary to hers. It is the dread of her exclusive and persecuting spirit, which she has always manifested when she has had the power, that makes enlightened Americans set their faces against her. She has been, ever since the development of the papacy, a persecuting Church, drunk with the blood of saints and martyrs, as the Waldenses and Albigenses can bear witness, as the *auto-da-fés* of your own native Spain, the massacre of the Reformed in the Low Countries under the gloomy bigot, Philip the Second, but too well prove."

"Can you name to me any doctrine or principle of the Church which makes it obligatory on her to call on the secular arm to suppress heresy or schism that uses no violence or physical force against her?"

"However that may be, her practice proves that she claims and exercises the right, and has the disposition to use it."

"Can you point me to an instance in which she has ever inflicted, or required to be inflicted, anything more than ecclesiastical censures and discipline on peaceable schismatics and heretics, who, in defence of their heresy or their schism use no other weapons than arguments drawn from reason, history, and the Holy Scriptures? If so, will you be so good as to name it?"

"I presume that there are many instances, but I cannot name one at this moment."

"No, nor at any other moment. I am not answerable for what civil or military governments have done. They have often violated the principles and wishes of the Church by their treatment of heretics. She never authorized the cruelties of

Henry VIII., in England, of the Duke of Alba, in the Netherlands, the revocation of the Edict of Nantes, or the dragonades of the Huguenots, by Louis the Fourteenth—the last ordered by the king during the suspension of his diplomatic relations with the Holy See. The Waldenses, after they desisted from violence towards the Church and her priests and members, were left in peace, and have remained unmolested to this day in the secluded valleys of Piedmont. The Albigenses were Manichæans, the descendants of the Paulicians, preaching the most licentious doctrines, and practicing moral and social abominations, such as are punishable by your own laws. They were not peaceable heretics; but, protected and supported by Raymond VII., Count of Thoulouse, took possession of the churches and their revenues, broke up peaceable congregations of worshipers, maltreated and murdered the clergy, and even assassinated a legate of the Holy See. The Pope called on the King of France, the Count's suzerain, for protection, and the king responded, and a bloody war followed against the Count, assisted, part of the time at least, by James of Arragon, who was under excommunication from the Pope. Suppose Brigham Young, chief of the Mormons—

whose well-known principle is, that the Lord has given to the Mormons all the possessions of the Gentiles, and that if they do not take them by force, it is because they are not yet strong enough to do it—should let loose his Danites to disturb peaceable Catholic congregations met for worship, should plunder Catholic churches, murder or otherwise maltreat Catholic priests, would not the American government hold itself bound to suppress the violence, and enforce the laws against him and his followers?"

"Undoubtedly, whether the misdeeds were committed against your Church or against any other Church."

"Precisely: now this is all that the Pope required of the secular arm against the Albigenses, in the south of France. That Simon de Montfort—who was appointed to lead the forces and execute the laws against the Albigenses, and who hoped to succeed to the possessions of Raymond—went beyond his instructions, turned the war into a war for his own personal aggrandizement, and committed cruel excesses and gross outrages on peaceable and inoffensive persons, even on helpless women and children, never intended either by the Pope or the king, is very certain, for the Pope withdrew the authorization he had given him, and under the direction of St. Dominic, established a court of inquiry, or inquisition, to protect the peaceable and well-disposed heretics from the excesses of the civil power."

This seemed conclusive enough, conceding the facts to be as the priest stated them. Whether they were so or not, I was not able to say; I could only say that Protestant historians give a very different account. According to them, the Albigenses were a numerous body of peaceful, evangelical Christians, who adhered to primitive Christianity, and maintained themselves in Gospel purity and free from papal corruptions and superstitions. But I do not know that Protestant historians, after all, are any better authority than Catholic historians. If the latter have an interest in white-washing, the former have an equally strong interest in black-washing the Church. The editor seemed to have nothing to reply, and changed the subject.

CHAPTER VIII.

"But you say nothing, Reverend Father, of the Spanish Inquisition and its two hundred and thirty thousand victims tortured and burned to death for daring to differ, on some abstruse questions, from the Pope of Rome. As a native-born Spaniard, I suppose you will defend it."

"Llorente, on whose authority you rely, was a native-born Spaniard, and he did not defend it, but circulated innumerable lies against it. He was a bad Spaniard, a bad priest, and a bad Catholic, and therefore worthy of the full confidence of the Reformed Communion. The Inquisition, as I have just told you, was originally instituted for the protection of heretics against the severity of the civil laws, which date from the pagan republic of Rome, from which the Church herself had suffered for centuries, and which she had no hand in making. The Christian Roman emperors, who never allowed the Church to interfere with their law-making power, sometimes suspended and sometimes renewed them, and the Barbarian nations, that succeeded the Romans, though they had certain laws and customs of their own, which were the law for Barbarians, continued in force for the Roman population the Roman law and jurisprudence. The Spanish Inquisition, of which many horrid tales—lies for the most part—are told, was a politico-ecclesiastical court, conceded by the Pope to the solicitations and representations of the kings of Spain, though reluctantly, and had for its object to ferret out and bring to trial, according to the judicial forms of the kingdom, persons accused or suspected of being engaged in secret conspiracies to overthrow in Spain both the Church and the state. These persons were, for the most part, recently baptized Jews and Mussulmans, who were suspected, while publicly professing themselves Christians, and in some instances filling high offices in the Church and in the state, of practising in secret their old religion, and plotting with the unbaptized Jews and Moors of Africa against the peace of the kingdom. I speak of the Spanish Inquisition in its origin. It was directed against real criminals, such as the laws of every civilized state treat, and, on conviction, punish as such."

"Do you mean to say the Inquisition was not

established to ferret out and bring to punishment persons held to be heretics?"

"The persons against whom it was instituted, doubtless were heretics, but it was not to ferret out and punish heretics, simply as such, that the Pope authorized the extraordinary court called the Inquisition, or that it was solicited by the kings, but against them as secret conspirators, threatening the destruction of Spanish society, both civil and religious, as it was then constituted. The court, in its first period, did not take cognizance of heresy when not suspected of being coupled with other offences."

"Will you say that no heretic, as such, and such only, was ever arrested and condemned by the Inquisition?"

"No, I will not say that; but I will say that it was not instituted or consented to by the Supreme Pontiff for that purpose."

"Were not persons suspected of favoring the Reformers in Germany and the Low Countries, arrested by the agents of the Inquisition, and thrown into its dungeons?"

"Undoubtedly: but that makes nothing against my position. You know, I presume, that the Reformers in Germany and the Low Countries, if not everywhere else, were not simply heretics in the eyes of the Church, but also a political party in the eyes of the state, and, as such, carried on in the Netherlands, then belonging to Spain, a civil war against their sovereign or suzerain. They were in the eyes of the Spanish government rebels and revolutionists, and no Spaniard could favor even their theological doctrines without suspicion of high treason. At least so it was represented to the Pope, who consented to the revival of the Inquisition under Philip II., and its extension to the Low Countries. That the Supreme Pontiff did not regard the suppression of heresy unconnected with a dangerous political party seeking to revolutionize the state as well as the Church, as its special purpose, is evident from the fact, that though there were many adherents of the Reformers—some open, and more concealed—in Naples, then an appanage to the Spanish crown, the Pope absolutely refused to consent to the introduction of the Inquisition into that kingdom."

"Do you maintain that no one guilty of no offence but what the Church calls heresy, was ever condemned by the Inquisition?"

"Not at all: I only say that this was not the purpose for which the Pope consented to its establishment, or re-establishment. That it was abused, and used for purposes not originally intended, we know from the letters of the Pontiff, seriously reprimanding the inquisitors for their severity and cruelty, and from his authorizing appeals from their sentences to the Papal court, where in most of the cases carried up, the sentences of the Inquisition were overruled, and the prisoners discharged. Besides, the two orders were so intermingled in Spain, that it was hardly possible that an offence could be committed against either order that would not be equally an offence against the other; and it is easy to conceive, that even after the adherents of the Reformers had ceased to couple their heresy with rebellion, or treasonable practices against the government—if in fact they ever did cease so to couple it in Spain—the Inquisition might construe the heresy as an offence of which it had cognizance."

"But whose fault was it that the two orders became so intermingled?"

"It was the fault of time. Many things are just and useful when adopted, that cease to be so, and indeed become positively hurtful, in process of time and the changes which it brings with it; yet to undo them, or to reform the abuses to which they have ultimately led, and which have become incorporated into the habits, the customs, the life of a people, and especially if they favor the secular government by giving it a *quasi* authority in ecclesiastical affairs, is a work of great difficulty and delicacy. '*Hic opus, hic labor est.*' The Popes had conceded many privileges to the Christian princes of Spain after the Mussulman invasion and conquest of nearly the whole kingdom, and the Christians were but a feeble remnant taking refuge in the mountains of the Asturias, and during the war against the Infidels for the recovery of the kingdom, which lasted nearly eight hundred years. These privileges strengthened the hands of the princes and of the Christian warriors, and served the interests of both religion and national independence. But when the war was ended, Granada had fallen, the last Mussulman prince expelled from the Iberian peninsula, and Spain was once more free and Christian, the order of things that had grown up during the long struggle for the Christian faith and national integrity ceased to be necessary or useful, and became in many respects positively injurious to both Church and state, and especially embarrassing to the Church. The king was found to have an undue authority in ecclesiastical matters; there was produced a sort of confusion of the two orders, for which Spain and Spanish America are now paying the penalty. I defend not that confusion of Church and State, which resulted from measures wise and just in their origin, nor do I defend throughout the Spanish Inquisition, always more political than ecclesiastical; but I cannot join in the ordinary outcry against either. I prefer, wherever practicable, the relations of Church and State which subsist in your republic."

"But did I not understand you to defend the union of Church and State in the Old World?"

"The *union*, yes; but not the *fusion* of Church and State, or the intermingling of the two authorities. The trouble in Spain was not, as you suppose, that the Church had too much power or independence, but that the government had gradually come to exercise an undue power in ecclesiastical appointments and ecclesiastical administration. The two authorities should always be kept distinct; and while the Church abstains from all interference in the administration of the purely temporal affairs of state, the secular government should have no authority in the administration of ecclesiastical affairs. The only union of Church and State, as polities or corporations, I have defended, is that implied by concordats which accord to the state certain specified rights and powers, and impose on it certain obligations with regard to ecclesiastical matters."

"If you express the views of your Church, I see not why she condemns those who advocate a separation of Church and State."

"I have already shown you why. In the Old World the state has never recognized the American doctrine. The state has remained always pagan, as you are laboring to make it here, and I fear successfully. It claimed the absolute supremacy in all things, and that the rights of the Church were held from it, or by its concession. It would concede her freedom only as the state religion, and as a state religion the state had, according to its theory of its own supremacy, the right to control its administration. This the Church could not, as a spiritual kingdom, permit; but as the state would concede her no rights save as the established religion of the state, she was obliged to acquiesce in her establishment by law, and to secure by law or treaty the best terms for herself that she could. To dissolve the treaty or abrogate the law, and thus separate her entirely from the state, would leave her without any rights at all, which the secular power holds itself bound to recognize."

"But what need, even supposing this to be so, had she to insist that the state should exclude, under the severest pains and penalties, all religions but herself? Simple protection from their violence would have answered her purpose as you pretend it does now."

"I am not aware that she ever did so insist. She had to accept her establishment as the state religion to be able to exercise any of her spiritual rights under the protection of law, and the state was too logical, when it had declared her the state religion, not to forbid all religions opposed to her. The laws against heretics grew naturally out of the supremacy claimed by the state, as under both the pagan republic and the pagan empire; and as that claim had never been acknowledged by the Church, she is in no sense responsible for the civil exclusion of heretics. You have only to study the controversies between the legists and the canonists during the struggle of the Pope and the Emperor in the Middle Ages, or between the canonists and the French parliaments in more recent times, to be satisfied that much of what you and men like you have attributed to the Church, is simply due to the arrogant and false claims of the secular order, always denied and resisted by the Church. The whole difficulty grew out of the assumption by the pagan state of supremacy, or its refusal to acknowledge an order of rights which you call the rights of man, and I the rights of the Creator, anterior and superior to itself, not derived from it, and which it is, as I so often repeat, bound to recognize and protect for all men. The Church was the guardian and defender of this order of rights against the tyranny of princes and civil magistrates."

"You would then claim for your Church the championship of liberty against tyranny, and boldly deny her despotic, tyrannical, and persecuting spirit?"

"Of course I do, and so would you, if you had studied her history, understood and approved the order of rights recognized and established by your own republic. The Church has always been on the side of true liberty, of justice, charity, humanity. He who defends against the arrogant pretensions of the secular order the rights of God, if I may so speak, defends the rights of man. You see, or would see, if your eyes were open, that the Popes, in defending the rights of the spiritual order against secular tyrants, were the real defenders of freedom, and the powerful opponents of the pagan republic or empire where liberty was restricted to the liberty of the state or city to govern; where the individual was nothing and the state everything. You would see it also, by what followed in those nations that, in the sixteenth century, threw off the papacy and rejected the authority of the Church. In them all, the secular authority was alike supreme in politics and in religion; and if there was liberty for the individual to blasphéme the Church and curse the Pope, there was no liberty for him to dissent from the religion of the state or the prince. Cardinal Fisher and Sir Thomas More, in England, were beheaded, because they would not subscribe to the declaration that the king was supreme in spirituals as well as temporals, and seventy-two priests were condemned to death and executed, and hundreds of laymen were doomed to death, and I know not how many more had their goods confiscated and were suffered to die in loathsome dungeons, or were banished the realm, under Queen Elizabeth, because they would not take the oath of the royal supremacy. The king and parliament enacted the creed and liturgy of the new-made Church of England, as they still do, and as did the princes or secular authority in every state that apostatized from the Church. It has cost these nations centuries of revolution and civil war to regain some portion of the liberty the Church had always defended for them. You, my dear friend, are a thorough pagan in your views of the relation of Church and State, and in your opposing the Church you are warring against the very idea of that freedom which the Church defends, and which makes the glory of your republic."

"The American republic is only the American people, and American liberty is simply liberty as they understand it; and the American people do not understand either civil or religious liberty in your sense, and they spurn the glory you would award them."

"I call the American republic the American people as organized by the Constitution and laws, and I place their glory in having recognized liberty as a spiritual right, not as a civil grant, and therefore of having identified it in principle with conscience, which is accountable to God alone; or in other words, in having founded their state on the principles of justice and equal rights, and therefore on the supremacy of the spiritual order, which the Church has always asserted and defended. That you do not see that making justice and equal rights, not civil grants, but the very basis of the state, is the assertion of the supremacy of the spiritual order, is very possible; that the American people are losing sight of it, and are resolving the sovereignty of the people into the sovereignty of popular opinion, is no doubt true, and to be deeply regretted. You are, as a people, no longer what you were even when I first became an American citizen, and you are changing every day, and, in an old man's judgment, for the worse. You are losing the sense of the great principles on which your fathers built, and no longer see or understand the deep significance of the providential constitution of your republic. You are perverting the Christian to the pagan republic. Hence your great need of the Church to recall your minds to the first principles of your institutions, and to enable you to inherit the glory of being the first nation that ever fully asserted spiritual freedom."

Here the conversation closed for the day. The editor was silent for the first time, and seemed thoughtful. For myself, I was confounded, and hardly dared trust my own ears. I had no more doubted that the Romish Church had been an arrogant and domineering, a cruel and persecuting Church, than I had doubted my own existence. Had I not in my infancy learned the *New-England Primer*—my father was a Puritan—and the story of John Rogers, and as I grew up had I not not read *Pilgrim's Progress*, and Fox's *Book of Martyrs?* Was I to be told all that I had been taught, and all I had read in history, against the Church of Rome was false and calumnious, and that the Pope, instead of being anti-Christ, had from the first been, in being the champion of the claims of the Church, the champion of freedom and humanity? This was too much. I could swallow much, but not this. Were all the great, learned, and pious men, who ought to have known what they said, and who had borne their testimony against her, been deceived, or willing to deceive others? No; it could not be.

And yet many more men, a hundred to one of them, equally great, equally learned, equally pious, equally distinguished, equally incapable of deceiving or of being deceived, had as directly and as explicitly borne their testimony in her favor. Here was this venerable priest, whose very face, and the tones of whose voice, won your confidence, and who seemed to know beforehand all the objections of the journalist, and was always prompt with his answer; could I doubt his knowledge or his sincerity? He seemed never to be taken by surprise, he seemed to shirk no difficulty, and to meet every question fairly and frankly. Had we all been mistaken? I wish the editor was better able to cope with the priest. Well, I am too old to trouble my head with so perplexing a question: I will dismiss it.

CHAPTER IX.

I DID not succeed in dismissing the subject from my mind, though I would not let it trouble me much. I had learned long ago to take life easy, and never to let anything seriously disturb it. I had not thought much of religion, and was not, though a New-Englander by birth and breeding, of an earnest character. I usually, after my father's death, attended the services of the Protestant Episcopal Church, for it was only decent to observe some form of worship, and the Episcopalian Church had a decorous service, and was a Church that an easy-going gentleman could attend. It did not pry into one's private character or private affairs, exacted not much of one's time or thought, and the minister, usually a well-bred man, of agreeable manners, and a good reader, edified his congregation with a gracefully written and delivered sermon, or moral essay, which tasked no one's credulity, and disturbed no one's conscience. So it was in my younger days; it is somewhat different now, I am told; but my pastor is of the old school, and distracts his people with none of the novelties which, since the beginning of the Tractarian movement, have disturbed the peace of the Church.

Yet the words of the priest had taken an unusual hold of me, and haunted me in spite of myself. They had not convinced me, but they had shaken me, and made me suspect that there might be another side to the story; so the next day, seeing the priest and the journalist apparently about to resume the conversation of yesterday, I drew near to listen, with more eagerness than I was in the habit of showing or even feeling. The journalist, as I came near, was saying:

"All that, Reverend Father, will do to tell to ignorant papists, who have been trained from infancy to swallow everything their priests say, but we all know that your Church claims to teach by authority, and that she allows no religious liberty. She tolerates no free thought, no free exercise of reason—that noblest prerogative of man—permits no one to think for himself, or to have and act on convictions of his own."

"Do not the adherents of the Reformers profess to teach by authority? Do they not assert the infallible authority of the Bible, and forbid any one to hold anything contrary thereto? How much more free thought or free thinking for one's self is there under an infallible book than under an infallible Church?"

"I am not bound by the Reformers. I honor them for the noble stand they took against the arrogance and despotism of Rome, and for having originated a movement which, in its onward progress, sweeps away the spiritual despotism of the papal Church, delivers the world from spiritual thraldom, secures religious liberty, regains the free exercise of reason, and vindicates the rights and dignity of human nature. Man can now be man, free and noble, not the trembling, crouching victim of priestcraft and superstition."

"Do you know all that, my dear journalist?"

"Certainly I do."

"You know a great deal, then, as becomes the chief editor of a leading metropolitan journal, which gives its opinions off-hand on every subject and some others. But are you, after all, quite sure that the Church proscribes reason, anathematizes free thought, and permits no one to think or act for himself."

"Quite sure."

"Then you are sure of much more than I am. I have never found myself forbidden to reason, and have never felt my freedom of thought restrained."

"You know well, Reverend Father, that the Church imposes on you a creed, all cut and dried, which you must believe, without ever being permitted any free examination of it, or to entertain any doubt of its truth. You have never been free to adopt any conclusion contrary to her authoritative teaching."

"Without falling into error, and exposing myself to the inevitable consequences of error, agreed; but have you?"

"Have I? I am free to examine all questions for myself, and to abide by the convictions of my own mind, whether they square with the teachings of the Church or not."

"Without danger of error, or of missing the truth?"

"My convictions—my honest convictions—are the truth for *me*."

"Truth, then, has no existence independent of one's own honest convictions. How, then, do you distinguish truth from falsehood? Nay, what distinction can there be? Men's convictions differ, and what is the truth for one may be falsehood for another. The same thing, then, may be both true and false, be and not be, at one and the same time. I admit I have never been free to believe that."

"In this world we can never know what truth is independent of us, nor that there is any truth but our own convictions. Freedom of thought, the free exercise of reason, the right to think for ourselves, means the recognition of the sufficiency of each one's own convictions for himself."

"That is, a man who always acts according to his own convictions of what is true or false, right or wrong, is morally irreproachable?"

"That is what I mean."

"So, if you had a real conviction that you ought to cut my throat, you would commit no wrong in doing so? Is that the conclusion at which you arrive by what you call the free exercise of reason?"

"My reason tells me that such an act would be wrong."

"Undoubtedly, because it tells you that there is a right, therefore a truth, not dependent on your convictions, to which your convictions themselves must conform in order to be true, or a safe rule of conduct."

"But every man has the natural right to the free exercise of his own mind in seeking the truth, and no one can believe contrary to his convictions."

"Nothing more true. But a man's convictions to-day may change to-morrow, and the truth which now contradicts them, may be in accordance with them, when he has changed them. I can not believe contrary to my convictions, for my convictions are my belief, for the time being; and it is very true that no one can believe what contradicts his reason. But things may appear to contradict reason, and therefore incredible, that in reality accord with reason. When the apparent contradiction is explained they become credible, and on sufficient testimony, or adequate authority, may be believed without any surrender of reason; nay, reason then requires them to be believed. Because in such cases I believe on the authority of the Church, am I deprived of the free exercise of my reason?"

"The Church tells you beforehand what you must and must not believe, and permits you no free inquiry after truth, and thus dwarfs or stunts the growth of the mind."

"That is to say, the mind grows and expands not by the possession of truth, but by the search after it! That is part and parcel of the doctrine of progress, which we disposed of some days ago. The body, according to you, it seems, is dwarfed or stunted in its growth, is rendered weak and sickly by having appropriate food, and grows, becomes strong and healthy by not having it, and by seeking and never finding it! Truth is the appropriate food of the mind, which pines away and dies of inanition without it. They who have the truth do not need to seek it—for one seeks only what one has not—and they who have it not are not only free, but bound to seek it with all diligence and perseverance. To you, and such as you, the Church not only permits but commands free inquiry. Your objection to the Church, then, is not well put."

"The Church begins with the child and prejudices it in the very outset against all views of truth but her own, so that never after can it inquire freely. The objection to her is, that she closes the mind, and does not leave it open to the reception of new views, new discoveries, nor encourage it to advance with ever-advancing science.'

"Something of that has already been considered. There is, my friend, a difference between us, which is not unnatural. You, finding that you have not the truth, and despairing of ever finding it, hold that the good thing is not the possession of truth, but the exertion the mind makes in seeking it; I, believing that the Church has taught me the truth from my infancy, hold that the good thing is in possessing it, and using it to make me and my fellow-men wiser and better. You assume that the Church teaches the child her *view* of truth—that is, a theory of truth; I hold that she teaches no view or theory of truth, but the truth itself. Supposing me to be right in this, your objection turns only against yourself. If the Church teaches the child the truth, she does not prejudice the child against truth, but simply arms it against error—a very wholesome prejudice, if prejudice it be. You, confessing that you have not yet attained to the knowledge of the truth, and therefore can have at best only a view or theory of truth, which, upon examination, may or may not turn out to be true, feel very naturally that any attempt to give the child instruction is to prejudice it against every view but the one presented, and thus to forestall its judgment. You are right on your hypothesis; but how on that hypothesis can you consistently give your child any instruction at all? It strikes me that you should leave the child's mind to grow up in as complete ignorance of religion and morality, as perfect a blank, as possible. This would exclude all parental instruction, all domestic education and discipline, all schools, colleges, and even universities, and forbid all efforts to 'train the young idea how to shoot.' It is your doctrine, not that of the Church, my dear journalist, that is hostile to thought, to education, to science and learning, and that fosters ignorance."

"I do not concede that what the Church teaches is true, and reject her dogmas as false and absurd, and her morality as repugnant to human nature."

"Without having ever examined either, or ascertained what they are?"

"I know them well."

"As misrepresented and perverted by the enemies of the Church."

"I reject her dogmas."

"On what authority?"

"On the authority of reason: no better authority is needed for a rational man."

"Do you say the dogmas of the Church contradict reason?"

"Certainly: her dogmas are unreasonable and absurd."

"Does that mean, in your vocabulary, anything more than that they do not lie in the plane of reason, and that by reason alone you are unable to see or demonstrate their truth?"

"It means that they are contrary to reason, and are intrinsically incredible."

"That is a serious assertion, and I presume you are ready to prove it."

"That is easy enough; but it would necessitate a sort of discussion for which I have no taste."

"I do not doubt it: besides, you shift your ground. You began by objecting to the Church—not as a theologian, but as a publicist—that she holds principles and authorizes practices dangerous to liberty, hostile to progress, and at war with modern civilization. This was a legitimate ground of objection for a secularist. You raised a question which we could discuss on a ground and decide by principles, common to us both."

"But I do the same when I object to the Church that she teaches doctrines contrary to reason, for we both admit the authority of reason."

"For all questions lying within the plane of reason; but for questions above that plane, reason has only a negative authority. The dogmas of the Church are, if anything, above reason; and if they do not contradict reason, it can judge neither of their truth nor their falsity."

"So you refuse to submit the dogmas of the Church to the tribunal of reason. That is precisely what I complain of."

"Their intrinsic truth or falsity, yes; because, if truths at all, they are truths not of reason, but of revelation. Yet the question, whether they contradict reason or not, and the further question, whether I have adequate authority for believing them to be divinely revealed or not, are both questions to be decided, when raised, at the tribunal of reason."

"But suppose I prove the dogmas contrary to Scripture, would not that be enough for my purpose?"

"No dogmas repugnant to the Holy Scriptures can be true; but the question whether the dogmas of the Church are or are not repugnant to the Holy Scriptures, is one I cannot discuss with you."

"Why not?"

"Because the Holy Scriptures were deposited with the Church, not with you, and you are not their authorized interpreter. Also, because I have a strong suspicion that you have as little respect for their authority as you have for the authority of the Church. You may or may not believe them as you understand them, but they probably weigh little with you in any other sense. My understanding of them may be very different from yours, and there is no authority we both accept, to decide between us which of us is right or which is wrong. Each of us might insist on his own understanding, and be unable to convince the other, and so we might dispute forever without settling anything."

"This, Reverend Father, is precisely my objection to your Church. She refuses to submit her dogmas to the test either of reason or the Scriptures. It is therefore I accuse her of opposing religious liberty, anathematizing reason, and denying the freedom of thought."

"The Church refuses to submit no question to the test of reason which is within the province of reason, and she would be false to reason if she submitted any other. Any doctrine that contradicts either Scripture or reason, she holds to be incredible and false. All I insist on is, that the doctrine must really, not apparently only, contradict one or the other, and that the Church is as high authority, to say the least, as my friend the journalist, for determining what does or does not contradict reason, what is or is not repugnant to the Holy Scriptures."

"My objection is that she violates the freedom

of the mind and true religious liberty, by imposing a creed which is not in the province of reason, and commands her members, on pain of eternal damnation, to believe dogmas, of the truth or falsity of which she herself teaches that reason is not competent to judge."

"Your objection, if valid against the Church, is equally valid against divine revelation itself; at least against the revelation of anything above the natural order. But I see not how what you allege, even if true, violates religious liberty. The dogmas and discipline of the Church are matters within the spiritual order, with which you, as a publicist, have nothing to do. You are not one of her members, and the law does not compel you to become a member, to hold her doctrines, or to submit to her discipline. No one is compelled to join her communion against his will; and would it accord with your notions of religious liberty to prevent by force those who would do so from joining her, or to use force to compel her to change either her doctrine or her discipline?"

CHAPTER X.

"It is a shame and a disgrace, that in this enlightened age, and in this free republic, a Church that teaches such antiquated and absurd dogmas, and exercises such despotic control over her members, should be suffered to exist."

"So you would suppress her by force, and outlaw all who adhere to her! You do not seem to have made much progress since the Reformers in your understanding of religious liberty. Do you call it religious liberty to deny me the right to belong to and defend the Church, while you are free to reject her and use force against her? This, I am aware, was the view of the Reformers in the sixteenth century, but I thought you had advanced beyond them. Are you not a little antiquated in your notions? or have you forgot your part, and supposed you were opposing, not defending, the freedom of religion?"

"There is no violation of religious liberty in warring against the Church. She is intrinsically a spiritual despotism. Such is the control she has over her ignorant and superstitious members, that few of them dare leave her communion."

"Well, what do you propose to do about it? Does not religious liberty mean the freedom of conscience? If my conscience requires me to believe what the Church teaches, and to submit to her discipline, what freedom of conscience have I if the state forbids me to do so, and punishes me with fine, imprisonment, exile, or death, if I follow my own conscience without disturbing others in the peaceful enjoyment of theirs? Do you boast of the equality of all men, and yet contend that I and my brethren have not an equal right with you and yours to the freedom of conscience? Whence do you derive any right of conscience which we have not?"

"The Church denies to men their natural freedom, and, by so doing, forfeits all right for herself, and justifies the use of force against her."

"So said the late Know-Nothing party, and therefore proposed to deprive Catholics of the right of citizenship. Had they succeeded, they probably would have gone so far as to prohibit any citizen, under pain of treason to the state, to give a Catholic either 'fire or water.' This would have been not much more than was done by some of the old colonial laws, which made it a highly penal offence to harbor a priest for a single night, or to give him even a single meal of victuals. Your countrymen, however, did not take kindly to the Know-Nothing party, except in a few localities, and have already nearly if not quite forgotten it. The doctrines and practices of the Church cannot be more offensive to you than the doctrines and practices of those outside of her communion are to her or to me; and if she bears with you, why cannot you bear with her? If you dislike her doctrine and worship, if you believe them despotic and degrading, are you not free to say so, and prove you are right if you can? What hinders you from using all your learning, wit, and science against her? Do you fear that in an open field and fair encounter she will get the better of you, and therefore require her to be bound hand and foot by the civil magistrate before you dare venture to enter the lists against her? If so, your confidence in your cause is far less than my confidence in mine."

"This would do very well if your Church held herself amenable to reason, but that she does not. A Church that will not reason can not be met by reason. She can be met only by force. She is exclusive, claims supremacy, will be all or nothing; and nothing, I say, let her be."

"So, while you recognize the equal rights as citizens under the protection of the laws of sectarians, Jews, Mahometans, pagans, and scoffers at all religion, you make an exception against the Church, and against her alone. Well, if you did but know it, the distinction you make is in the highest degree honorable to her, and proves that she must have a merit none of them can pretend to. But let us examine your reasons for excepting the Church from the equal rights on which your republic is based."

"Do you deny that she refuses to hold herself amenable to reason?"

"Certainly I do, and energetically. She holds the truth or falsity of her doctrines is above the plane of reason, but she concedes that her children should have the highest and best of all reasons for believing them. Things which contradict reason are incredible and false, as I have already told you; but things may be above reason, the intrinsic truth or falsity of which lies beyond the direct apprehension of reason, and yet not be contrary to reason. These things, accredited by adequate testimony, are credible, and reason herself requires us to believe them. The dogmas of the Church are received and believed because God, who can neither deceive nor be deceived, has revealed them. I can not raise the question whether what he reveals is true or not. What he reveals is his word, and his word is truth. There is and can be no better or higher reason for believing anything than the fact that God says it."

"Than the *fact* that he says it; but that fact must be proved. You have no proof of it; you simply take it on the authority of the Church, and have only her word for it."

"If God has instituted the Church, made her the witness and keeper of his revelation, and commissioned her to go into all the earth and teach it to every creature, to all men and nations; and if he remains ever present with her, assisting her to teach it, and supernaturally guarding her against the possibility of error in teaching it, her word is amply sufficient to accredit the fact of revelation, all the demands of reason are complied with, and my faith is in the highest sense reasonable. The divine commission to teach warrants the infallibility of the commissioned in teaching, for God can not authorize the teaching of error."

"The fact of the divine commission to teach the word of God, must itself be proved, not assumed."

"Agreed. The Church has always claimed it, and there is not and never has been a rival claimant. Her claim was made in the time of the apostles, and down to the sixteenth century was admitted by the whole Christian world, and is still admitted by the immense majority of all who bear the Christian name; by all, indeed, except those whom she condemns as heretics, and even they admitted it before she condemned them. She has the right, then, to plead possession, prescription, and it is for those who deny that she is rightfully in possession, to show good and valid reasons why she should be ousted, or her claim be set aside.

"Do you mean to assert that the Eastern Churches have always admitted and still admit the infallible authority of the Church in teaching?"

"Certainly I do. They hold as firmly as I do the divine and infallible authority of the Church to teach all men and nations the revelation of God. There is no dispute between them and the Western Church as to the authority of the Church. The Oriental Churches not in communion with the Roman See, simply deny that the supreme authority is vested in the Bishop of Rome, and assert that it is vested in the general council of bishops. Yet they hold that it is essential to a general council and the validity of its acts that it be convoked and presided over by the Roman pontiff, in person or by his legates, and that its acts be approved by him. The only nominal Christians worth counting, who deny the infallibility of the Church in matters of faith and morals, are the adherents of the Reformers in the sixteenth century, commonly called Protestants. They have all the rest of Christendom against them."

"Prescription may be a good title in law, or in matters where absolute right is impracticable, and can be only approximated; but in matters of faith, where absolute truth is assumed to be necessary, if presumptive proof, it certainly is not conclusive."

"It is only as presumptive proof that I urge it. Yet in the present case it is really conclusive. There is no moment of time since the apostles, that the claim has not been made, conceded, and acted on. It must then have an apostolic origin; and if of apostolic origin, the question is settled, since the Church is founded on the apostles, Jesus Christ himself being the chief corner-stone."

"The claim of the Church was vicious in its origin, and prescription avails nothing. No such commission ever issued."

"The presumption is against you, and the *onus probandi* is on you; prove what you allege, and you will unquestionably unchurch the Church. But how will you prove it? Do you set up a counter-claim for yourself or the Reformation?"

"No. Have I not just said that no commission was issued."

"Then, of course, neither you nor the sects that sprung from the Reformation, have any infallible authority or divine commission to teach?"

"We claim none. We have not the arrogance and presumption of Rome."

"Then neither you nor they are any authority against the Church. You at best are confessedly fallible, and she at worst can be only fallible. Her chances, at the very lowest of being right, are equal to yours at the very highest. You must, then, support your denial by proof, or it will count for nothing."

"The Church can not be infallible, if she contradicts herself; teaches one thing to-day and another and a contradictory doctrine to-morrow."

"Certainly not. But she has never done so, and you are hardly free, till you retract the charge you began by preferring, to maintain that she has."

"Whether she has or has not contradicted herself, is a purely historical question; and history presents us the scandal of councils contradicting councils, popes contradicting councils, and councils contradicting popes."

"So says Chillingworth; but so says not history in any sense to your purpose. The infallibility of the Church is not universal, but extends only to the things covered by the commission, in the words of our Lord, 'All things whatsoever I have commanded you.' It is not claimed that it is commensurate with her authority, or that she is infallible except in teaching the revealed truth, and in judging what does or does not accord with it. Disciplinary canons are obligatory, but not necessarily infallible; and the infallibility of the Church is restricted to her doctrinal canons, or her dogmatic definitions; definitions either declaring what the faith is, or what it is not; that is, condemning what is opposed to it."

"Very well. I understand all that."

"The Church speaks infallibly only when she speaks in her unity and integrity, that is, through an Œcumenical Council, or through her Supreme Pontiff, Vicar of Christ, and successor of Peter in apostolical authority. Theologians add a third way, the *ecclesia dispersa*, or the bishops dispersed, and each in communion with the Pope, teaching in his own particular diocese; but as we can know only through the Pope or an Œcumenical Council, what these bishops dispersed throughout the whole world agree in teaching and believing, I need not count it. Now, in order to sustain your assertion, you must produce an instance of an Œcumenical Council contradicting the dogmatic teaching of another Œcumenical Council or a Pope, and of a Pope contradicting the dogmatic teaching of an Œcumenical Council or another Pope or Supreme Pontiff. Can you produce an instance?"

"I can find instances enough. The Council of Nicæa differed from the Council of Antioch. Pope Liberius, after his return from exile, condemned the acts and the fathers of the Council of Rimini; the Council of Chalcedon and the Pope both contradicted the second Council of Ephesus, in regard to the monophysite doctrine of Eutyches; a council and a Pope both censure Pope Honorius as a fautor of the monothelite heresy; and there were several councils that condemned the keeping and worshiping of images, and others that approved it. Many more instances, I doubt not, might be adduced, but these are enough to prove what I have said."

"Yet, unhappily for your argument, not one of them is historically true, or if true, to your purpose. There was no Œcumenical Council of Antioch, and therefore its acts were not contradicted by the Council of Nicæa. The Council of Rimini was no Œcumenical Council, and the acts of the bishops assembled, who were grossly maltreated by the Arian Emperor, had no validity, for St. Liberius refused to approve, and in fact, as you allege, condemned them. There was no *second* Council of Ephesus, and so there could be no contradiction between it and Chalcedon. There was an irregular and tumultuous assembly, commonly called the *latrocinium* of Ephesus, but its acts were instantly condemned by the Pope, St. Leo the Great, and were never accounted of any authority either in the East or in the West. No council or Pope ever condemned any dogmatic decision of Pope Honorius, and he was censured after his death, not for his faith, which was orthodox, but for having favored the monothelite heresy by his culpable negligence in not suppressing it. No council, general or particular, ever approved what you call the *worship* of images, and no general council ever condemned the keeping and honoring sacred images and pictures for the worth to which they are related. The assemblies convoked by the iconoclastic Emperors of Byzantium, that condemned them, had no authority to speak in the name of the Church. There is no instance on record, or producible, of any dogmatic contradiction between one Pope and another, or between a Pope and a General or Œcumenical Council."

"It is easy to get rid of contradictions in your way; you have only to declare one of the contradictors an irregular assembly, or no council, and the work is done."

"The sneer is misplaced. The General Council is a regular body, and must be convoked by the Pope, or with his consent; it must be presided over by the Roman Pontiff in person or by his legates, and its acts must be approved by the Pope, as must the acts of your Congress by your President. So it is ordained by the ancient canons, admitted by the East and the West, and hence the schismatic Greeks confess to this day their inability to hold an Œcumenical Council, because such a council can be held only under the presidency of the Archbishop of Rome."

"Let the Greeks go ; they are no better than the Romanists. But because no instance of dogmatic contradiction has been produced, we cannot say none exists."

"But you must produce it before you can argue from it against the infallibility of the Church. If there were any such, we should have had it produced by the enemies of the Church before this. Your learned divines have ransacked every nook and corner of history to find a well-authenticated instance of the kind, and have failed, and now very generally, like yourself, bring the contrary charge, that she is unprogressive, and teaches always the same dogmas, and claims always the same anthority."

It struck me that the priest here made a strong point, and if borne out by the facts of the case, the charge of the editor, that the Church does not hold herself amenable to reason, and is therefore a spiritual despotism which may be suppressed in the name of religious liberty, is not, sustained. Certainly the Reformers did claim the right to use force against her, and as far as I recollect my reading, there was no instance in which the Reformation gained an establishment, except by the aid of the civil authority; and wherever it gained over the civil authority, it prohibited the Church, forbade Catholic worship, and punished adherence to it with fines, imprisonment, exile, and death. The state confiscated the revenues of the old religion, demolished or took possession of its churches, abbeys and priories, schools, colleges, universities, libraries, hospitals, foundations for the poor and the infirm, and carried on a wholesale system of robbery and plunder, and in some countries of wholesale massacre; as for instance, in Sweden, under Gustavus Vasa.

These things always pained me, but I had supposed them excusable, if not justifiable, by the fact that the old Church was a spiritual despotism, the common enemy of God and man. So on the same ground I had defended the European Liberals in their violence to the Church, who, wherever they attain to power, use it to abolish her, as in the French revolution, or to restrict her, as in Italy, Austria, and Spain. But if what the priest says be true, the Church is no spiritual despotism, and offers no violence to reason, but gives the highest and best of all reasons for the authority she claims, and the truth of what she teaches.

Surely things may be above reason, or suprarational without being against reason or contrarational. Human reason is not unlimited, and who dares say that nothing exists of which reason can not take cognizance, or that the limits of reason are the limits of reality? This is a question which affects Protestants no less than it does Catholics, and no one felt it more strongly than Luther, who even represents, as I am told, reason as worthless. Whoever professes to believe in the Christian mysteries, whether he believes them on the authority of the Church or of the Bible, professes to believe in the suprarational, or truths above reason. The mysteries of the Trinity, the Incarnation, the vicarious Atonement and Sacrifice, Redemption, Election, Regeneration, the relation of the regenerated soul to Christ, or the Holy Catholic Church, the Communion of Saints, the Resurrection of the Flesh, and Eternal Life, are all above reason; and if nothing above reason can be believed without denying and rejecting reason, nothing distinctively Christian can be believed.

Whether God has revealed these mysteries or not, is a question of fact; and if the fact be duly accredited, to believe it is as reasonable as to believe any fact on competent and sufficient testimony. There are thousands of things which we

LIBERALISM AND THE CHURCH. 147

all believe on testimony, that is, simply on authority; and do I reject reason when, on the authority of history, I believe there was such a man as Julius Cæsar, or that he was assassinated in the senate-chamber? Is belief on adequate authority never a reasonable belief? Nobody can pretend it. Then suppose the mysteries are simply above reason, not against reason, they are not incredible *à priori*, and on adequate authority or testimony, may be as readily and as reasonably believed as any other facts that rest on testimony. No testimony, less than the direct testimony, or word of God, could suffice to prove directly their truth; but all that is needed to be proved is the fact that God has revealed them; their truth follows from the fact that God, who reveals them, can not lie, and is truth itself; and to prove the fact that God has revealed them, ordinary historical testimony suffices.

Clearly, then, the editor was hasty in declaring that the Church refuses to reason. If the facts are as the priest stated, his conclusion is logical, and can not be gainsaid. There can be no doubt that the Divine commission to teach carries with it the Divine pledge of the infallibility of the commissioned in all things covered by the commission. If the commission was issued to the Church—to the Papal Church—her infallibility follows as a simple logical sequence, as does the truth of all she teaches as divine revelation. Suppose the facts, the conclusion is irresistible. But was the commission ever issued? was it issued to the apostles and their successors, and is the Papal Church their legitimate successor? These are the points to be proved, and if proved, the controversy is ended with all who can and dare reason. Is it Protestants, then, who reject reason?

CHAPTER XI.

THE journalist saw nothing in the priest's answer to accept or deny. He could and would on no consideration whatever accept the infallibility of the Church. He did not profess to be a philosopher or a theologian, and seemed to regard a publicist as perfectly competent to sit in judgment on either. I who, perhaps, had first and last picked up here and there far more knowledge of ecclesiastical history than he could boast, felt myself, while reluctant to admit the priest's reading of history, quite too ignorant to pronounce him wrong. But the editor proceeded as if all statements that went beyond his knowledge, or against his theories, could be only a fable or a cunning invention. What struck me most in him was his apparent inability to recognize common sense or common honesty in the adherents of the old religion. He seemed to suppose them all knaves or fools, devoured on the one hand by a crafty and intriguing spirit, and on the other degraded by the grossest ignorance, superstition, and slavishness. He believed this was the only effect to be looked for from the Church, and therefore he would keep no terms with her. Indifferent to all else, he was deadly hostile to the Pope and Catholicity. He replied:

"Be all that, Reverend Father, as it may, I still insist that your Church is hostile to freedom of thought, to the use of reason, and to religious liberty. She professes to be the kingdom of God on earth, to have the right to govern all men and nations, and to be invested with absolute authority over reason and conscience. In joining her communion, you surrender both to her dictation, and are no longer free to say your soul is your own. You part with your very manhood, and become an abject slave."

"It is singular that I have never, during my long life, discovered that alleged fact. I have always felt and acted as a freeman, as I have already told you."

"That is because her chains have eaten into your very soul, and you are a slave without knowing it. You know you are not free to believe as your own reason dictates, and must defend the opinions your Church bids you defend."

"I am a slave, as St. Paul said he was a slave, to Jesus Christ, and glory in it, for slavery to him is true freedom—a freedom which none separated from him or his Church ever enjoy or have any conception of. You, my dear Journalist, have yet to learn that all real freedom is in subjection to God. They who do not submit themselves, body and soul, to Him to whom they belong, have no true liberty, but are veritable slaves of doubt and uncertainty, of ignorance and error, or of their own passions and lusts. It is the truth, not error, that makes free."

"The Church denies you the liberty of forming your own opinions; you are obliged to accept hers on pain of eternal exclusion from heaven."

"You labor under a slight mistake, my philosophical friend. The Church teaches and enjoins no opinions. According to her doctrine, as I have learned it, opinions are free, and she in no degree restricts them in anything which is a matter of opinion, or on which the truth is not revealed or known."

"But you are not free to form your own opinions."

"Why not? What restrains me? Perhaps there is a little misunderstanding between us.

You demand freedom to form your own opinions: may I ask on what subjects?"

"On all subjects."

"Are you free to form opinions on subjects on which you know the truth, and are certain? Take the axioms of mathematics, and the definitions of geometry; are you free to form your own opinions concerning them? Is it a matter of opinion that the sun, whose golden rays we see gilding yonder mountain-top, is approaching the western horizon? Is it a matter of opinion that the three angles of a triangle are equal to two right angles?"

"No; these are matters of science or of sight. I know them, and assert them as facts of knowledge, not as opinions."

"Then where you know the truth, and are certain, you are not free to form your own opinions, for there is no room for any opinion at all. Then you are and demand to be free to form your own opinions only where you are ignorant and uncertain of the truth?"

"That is all."

"Well, my dear free-thinking friend, I have all the freedom that you have or ask for. Where the Church does not teach me the truth, put me in possession of the knowledge of the truth, she leaves me free to form and follow my own opinions. I am, then, at least as free as you are; besides I may, possibly, have much knowledge of truth which you have not."

"But, if you form, utter, or act on opinions contrary to what she teaches, she condemns and punishes you as a heretic."

"Not if I do it ignorantly and in good faith, not knowing what on the points on which I err she really teaches; but if I do know what she teaches, and thus know the truth, there is, as we have seen, no matter of opinion in the case. We can form opinions only where we do not know the truth, and are doubtful where it lies. The Church does not impose opinions, she teaches the truth. Your misapprehension grows out of your assumption that all theological doctrines are simply opinions. They really are so with you, who substitute opinion for faith, and therefore you conclude they must be so with the Church and with all who receive her as their teacher. Hence you suppose that in submitting to her authority, I am deprived of my freedom of mind, the use of my reason, the liberty of forming my own opinions, and therefore am in spiritual bondage, under a degrading and spiritual despotism."

"Certainly; that is my view."

"But as you are not infallible, it is possible that you are wrong. The Church does no violence to my reason or understanding in exacting my belief in or assent to the creed she teaches, any more than the mathematician does in exacting my assent to his axioms or his demonstrations, because the creed is the truth, received on the veracity of God revealing it, not an opinion which may or may not be true."

"Authority commands, it does not reason. You feel yourself bound to believe what the Church teaches, but this sense of obligation is not a rational conviction. Authority may silence reason, but does not convince it. It may well happen, that if you exercise your reason, it will dictate one thing while the Church commands you to believe another. Yet you must submit and refuse to follow or hear your own reason. This is why I term your Church a spiritual despotism, and denounce her as the enemy of reason, and the grave of all free thought."

"The internal conflict between reason and the Church in the bosom of her members, which you suppose, is impossible, if they know the grounds of their faith, and all may know them. I have all my life thought and reasoned as freely as most men; I have read and studied the substance of all that sectarians, Jews, infidels, rationalists, naturalists, pantheists, and atheists, have written against the Church, and I believe I am ignorant of no important objection urged from any quarter against her; and yet I have never for a moment found her and my reason in conflict, for my reason has always assured me that nothing is or can be more reasonable than to believe on the authority of God's revealed word duly accredited as his word."

"You have only the word of your Church, composed of fallible men, that what you are required to believe is the revealed word of God."

"I have the testimony of a divinely instituted, commissioned, and assisted body, reaching in unbroken unity and continuity from our Lord and his apostles down to me, to be the witness of the fact of revelation, and therefore a witness amply competent to accredit it to me and to all men and nations. In believing what the Church teaches, I believe the word of God, and am satisfied, as thoroughly convinced, as I could be by any demonstration in Euclid."

"You forget that I have denied the fact of the Divine commission."

"I do not forget it, but I do not heed it. You

gave no valid reason for your denial. You are confessedly fallible, and your denial, made on no authority, can have no value."

"But have you no authority for asserting the Divine commission but my alleged inability to disprove it?"

"I have. But in a discussion with you, the reasons I have already assigned, and which I need not repeat, are amply sufficient. The fact of the historical continuity of the Church from the apostles to us, always claiming it, professedly acting under it, and having her claim from the first conceded, is enough for any reasonable man. To a believer I could give additional and even stronger reasons, drawn from the very nature and design of Christianity as the means of the redemption, moral and spiritual progress, and final beatitude of the human race, but what I have said must suffice, unless you take avowedly the ground of rationalism or naturalism."

"Suppose I should take that ground, what would you do? Many, even amongst Protestants, have maintained that Protestantism is illogical, and inconsistent with itself; either too much or too little; too much, if God has made no revelation, too little, if he has; for it leaves us without any certain means of determining what it is he has revealed, which it is derogatory from the character of God to suppose he either could or would do. There is no question that Protestantism leaves all Protestants who think in doubt and uncertainty as to what God has revealed, if he has revealed anything. I have no sympathy with the Church, but I own it has a logical consistency with itself that Protestantism, as a system of religion, has not. I adhere to the Reformation, not for its doctrines, but as the uprising of the human mind against the intolerable despotism of Rome. But what have you to say in defence of your Church against one who takes the ground of rationalism or pure naturalism?"

"To one who takes it by way of argument or banter, nothing; to one who takes it seriously, I should have much to say. I would undertake to convince him, by arguments he could not deny, that neither nature nor reason suffices for itself; that nothing is more unnatural than naturalism, or irrational than rationalism; that neither does or can explain either the origin or the end of the universe in general, or of man in particular. Then I would show him that the natural is impossible without the supernatural, and that reason can not, by her own light or revelation, solve her own problems. Having shown this, I would proceed to show him that revelation is possible, is in accordance with the order of Divine Providence as manifested in nature, and therefore capable of being accredited by ordinary testimony. After that I would prove to him the historical fact of revelation, that it was made to man in the beginning, and that in no age or nation has man ever been left entirely without it; and close my argument by showing him that the revelation made in the Garden, and in substance the only revelation that has ever been made to man, is identically the Christian revelation transmitted through the patriarchs and the synagogue, preserved and taught in its purity and integrity by the Catholic Church. This would cover the whole ground, and meet all the objections of every class of objectors, from whatever point of view they object."

"I will not put you to the trouble of doing that, Reverend Father. I really do not take interest enough in the question to discuss it, or to listen to its discussion. All I demand is free, untrammeled thought for myself and for all men and on all subjects. Your Church does not allow it, and therefore I hold every true man should oppose her, and do his best to make away with her."

"Do you demand free thought so as to be able to arrive at the truth?"

"I demand it so as to be able to exercise and develop my faculties as a man, and not be kept always in leading-strings as a child."

"Still, I presume, you would like to think wisely and justly. We have agreed that truth is something real, independent of us, and that there is the right to which we ought to conform our thoughts, words, and deeds. Are you under no obligation to do the right when you know it, or to believe the truth when made known to you?"

"I regard all authoritative teaching, in matters of religion, as hostile to religious liberty; what I believe or disbelieve makes no difference. I say with Pope, nominally at least, a member of your own Church:

> 'For modes of faith let graceless bigots fight,
> 'His can't be wrong whose life is in the right.'

The important thing is, not what a man thinks or believes, but what he does."

CHAPTER XII.

I WAS sorry that the editor did not give the priest the opportunity to develop and establish his several points in defence of the Church against rationalism; but it was clear that however deep the editor's hostility to all authoritative teaching, he was really indifferent to all religion, and had no wish to believe in any. The only thing that he seemed in earnest about, was to get rid for himself and others of all positive belief of any kind. He had no serious convictions, and no earnest desire to know and believe the truth. It seemed clear to me that he thought he had an advantage of the priest, and that he was disposed to press it. There is no denying that the Church does claim to teach by authority, and to govern in spiritual matters her own members; and this age and country hold all authority in horror, and call it, however legitimate, just, and necessary, despotism. The journalist would recognize no distinction between just and unjust authority. All authority, in that it is authority, was for him despotism, and destructive of liberty. He would have no restraint in thought, word, or deed placed on any one; but every one should be free to live as he lists, unless, perchance, he adhered to the Catholic Church. He understood perfectly that the priest could not and would not concede this unbounded license, and thought, if he could only force him to deny it, he could then raise the cry of despotism against the Church with some appearance of justice, or with some plausibility. I was not pleased with him; for the principle of authority in matters of faith no man who believes in revelation at all can deny. We Protestants hold the principle of authority in faith as really as Catholics do, only we believe the authority on which we are to receive the revelation is the Bible, the infallible witness of what God has revealed, while Catholics hold that the authority, the infallible witness, is the Church.

But is it, after all, more difficult for Catholics to prove the infallibility of the Church than it is for us to prove the infallible authority of the Scriptures? The Bible is authoritative, because written by men divinely inspired to write it. How do I prove their inspiration? By the miracles of our Lord and his apostles. But how can miracles prove that? None but God can work a real miracle, and miracles therefore simply accredit those in whose behalf they are wrought as messengers from God, who could not work them unless God were with them, and God could not work miracles to accredit false witnesses or lying messengers. They are the seal of the divine commission that God gives to his messengers, or ambassadors, to speak in his name. Then if those thus accredited say they are inspired to reveal his Word, they are so. We believe the writers of the Holy Scriptures were inspired, because, being divinely accredited as his messengers, they are so. We must, then, prove the divine commission of the apostles, before we can prove they were inspired, or that the Sacred Scriptures were written by divine inspiration. All rests, then, on the fact of the divine commission of the apostles. With us, as well as with Catholics, this is the vital element. They, then, to prove the infallibility of the Church, have to prove only the same fact that we must prove in order to prove the infallibility of the Bible. If they can prove, as they say they can, that their Church is apostolic, that it continues without break the apostolate, its word is as high authority for what God has revealed as is the Bible itself, and the faith of Catholics is as reasonable, to say the least, as that of Protestants. I must think of this.

"You hold, then," replied the priest, "that it makes no difference what a man believes, if his life is in the right. Would what would be a right life in a pig, be a right life in a man?"

"Not at all; for man is the superior animal."

"Would it make no difference in regard to his life, whether a man believed as you do, or on the contrary, that the life of the pig is the proper human life?"

"Perhaps it would."

"Then it is not a matter of absolute indifference what a man believes. Man has, you have conceded, a moral nature, and therefore moral relations—relations to his Creator, to his neighbor, to society, and to the state. If so, he has certain duties as well as rights, which grow out of these several relations. Is the life of him in the right who neglects these duties, pays no attention to them, denies that he is under any obligation to perform them, that his neighbor has any rights he is bound to respect, and insists on his right to live as he lists?"

"I say not that."

"After all, is a man's life, on the whole, anything but a more or less imperfect practical application of his belief and that of the community in which he lives? I leave out, of course, exceptional characters, great rogues and great criminals, who are the slaves of untamed passions, and yet even these are not uniformly wicked in their whole lives, and perhaps the larger portion of their lives is inoffensive. I speak only of the generality of men."

"I have known atheists whose conduct might shame many Christians."

"But they had been born and bred in a Christian community, and formed under the influence of Christian morals, manners, customs, and civilization. The habits of early life remain and influence the conduct after the faith which formed them is gone. This is no fair test. The fair test would be to take, if you could find one, a nation of atheists, with only atheistical traditions, trained under atheistical influences, without regard to moral obligation, living without restraint, and with no other rule of conduct than the calculations of interest, or the impulses of passion."

"I do not deny morality, nor the obligations of duty."

"If you concede moral obligations you must assert the existence of God, for only God can impose an obligation. Human laws derive all their vigor as laws, from the law of God, which is his own eternal will or reason. There can be no moral obligation without a moral law, and creatures do not and can not create the moral law, for it is above them, and prescribes to them what they ought and what they ought not to do."

"But they may be a law unto themselves."

"Yes; if God has placed his law in their reason and instincts, and written it in their hearts, not otherwise. But even if so, it is none the less a law ordained by the Legislator who has the right over them, and to prescribe their conduct. A man is no less bound by the dictates of reason than by the precepts of an external law. Sins against the dictates of reason are the least excusable of all sins. Without God, then, no moral law; without the moral law, no moral obligation, no morality; without morality, based on the moral law, no state, no wise or just politics. Does it make no difference, then, whether men believe in God or deny him, and hold themselves accountable for their conduct in the several relations of life, or not?"

"But that does not prove that in order to

determine what is a proper human life, it is necessary to know and believe all the dogmas your Church teaches."

"All in good time. It is necessary to believe in God. Is it less necessary that we should, as far as concerns our relations to him, believe what is true of him, or will it answer as well to believe what is not true?"

"Proceed: say, what is true."

"Then it will be necessary to know or believe our true and real relation to him, the fact that he creates us, the end for which he creates us, the law under which he places us; also, our true relations to the rest of his creatures, to nature or the external universe, to our fellow-men, or to one another, as husband and wife, parent and child, brother and sister, neighbors, citizens or subjects, magistrates or rulers."

"Be it so."

"No less important or necessary will it be that we understand what are, and how we are to use, the true and efficient means of discharging the religious, moral, domestic, social, and political duties that grow out of our several relations in life—of fulfilling the law under which we are placed, and gaining the end for which we are made."

"Be it so, again."

"Well, my dear Journalist, the principles, the dogmas, the teachings of the Church go no farther than this; they only cover the several points on which every one in his degree and according to his state in life, needs to be rightly instructed from earliest childhood, if his life is to be in the right. Your mistake, my dear sir, as that of many others, arises from your not perceiving the practical character of the dogmatic teaching of the Church, and from supposing that her dogmas are merely speculative opinions, which have and can have no practical bearing on the real business of life. Hence your disdain or contempt of theology, and the disgust with which you look on the earnestness and warmth with which theologians discuss what to you are idle or senseless questions. Gibbon somewhere says with a sneer, in relation to the discussion between the Homoousians and the Homoiousians, the Christian world, for a hundred years, disputed and cut each others' throats for a single diphthong. True; yet in that diphthong was involved the whole question, whether the human race, after three hundred years of martyrdom, and when just emerging from the catacombs, was to be replunged into the idolatry, superstition, and barbarism of effete heathenism, or to go forward to the light and glory, the peace and happiness of Christian worship and Christian civilization. The whole future of humanity in this world and the next was at stake. The Athanasians, the Catholics, were the party of the future, of progress, of truth, of Christian civilization; the Arians were the party of the past, seeking to retain the human race in the bonds of heathen error, superstition and idolatry; for like the heathen they paid divine honors to one they held to be not God but a creature. Theological disputes you see, my worthy journalist, that seem to you trifling, nonsensical even, may, nevertheless, have a deep significance, and involve the gravest practical consequences. It is a sad proof of modern progress, the low rank you liberals or rationalists assign to theological science. They were deeper and sounder thinkers, and wiser men, who called theology "the Queen of the Sciences."

"But, Reverend Father, you seem to have changed sides, and to have become the advocate of progress, the champion of the future."

"No more than I have been all along. It is you and your friends, my dear sir, who are the enemies of progress. You seek to deprive humanity of all it has accumulated by the labors of all past generations, to reduce it to utter nakedness, and turn it out into a bleak and wintry world to starve, freeze, and die. I would preserve all that has been gained, and especially the living principles and practical truths, without which there may be destruction, but no progress, because no continuity of life. You and the party you sympathize with would render progress impossible if you could have your own way; for you would place the human race back in the darkness and slavery from which the Church has rescued it with so much toil and suffering, and by so many martyrdoms. You tell us nothing the world has not known and tried before the advent of our Lord, except what you have borrowed from the Church herself. You have borrowed, indeed, from her the very idea of progress, of which you will find no recognition in the writings even of the most eminent of Gentile philosophers, and you will seek in vain in the Gentile world for any practical progress, unless in the material order. The Gentile nations had all the nature that we have, and yet their moral, and intellectual, and social progress, was null. Their religious history is a history of a continuous deterioration, and the noble truths which you find in a Plato or a Cicero, were not new discoveries or new developments, but confessedly borrowed from the wisdom of the ancients, and which later generations had forgotten or obscured. You see repeated the same history in China, in Turkey, in all contemporary pagan and Mohamedan states and nations. Christian nations alone are living and progressive nations. And never have Christian nations advanced in all that makes the true glory of civilization so rapidly as they did from the downfall of Rome to the rise of what you call the Reformation.

"The reason of this," continued the priest, "is plain enough. The Church is always present in these nations, asserting the principles, and the means and conditions of all true progress, and aiding in their application to individual, social, and political life. She furnishes the principles, and assists in their continuous explication and application. Here is the reason why Christian nations, truly such, are living and progressive nations, and why non-Christian nations are neither living nor progressive. All heresies and infidelity are disintegrating and destructive, if you will, but really hostile to progress. They interrupt the work of the Church, they interpose obstacles to her influence, deny or obscure the principles of progress, and as far as their power extends, so prevent their development and practical application, and not only peril souls, but hinder or retard the progress of civilization. Heretical nations are running the same career the ancient Gentile nations ran, and their influence, aided by the flesh, the world, and the devil, extends even to orthodox nations, and neutralizes, to a fearful extent, the power of the Church to apply her principles to her own children, so that these nations become almost as unprogressive as heretical nations themselves.

"I defend," concluded the priest, "progress, but by preserving the principles and institutions by which it is effected; I accept the New, joyfully and gratefully, so far as it grows out of the Old, and is but its development and application under the law prescribed by the true end of man. I war against what the liberals call new, because it is not new, but a revival of what the race has outgrown and thrown off, and because it tends only to destroy all that has been gained during the last eighteen hundred years. You do not and will not believe me, for you are bent on restoring defunct paganism, though you perhaps know it not. But events are rapidly proving that I am right. Religion is' fast losing its hold on the new generation; reverence for the wisdom of the past, the experience of ages, and the universal convictions of mankind, is well nigh gone, and it seems to be taken for granted that our fathers were all old fogies, and that all wisdom was born with us. The youth of every nation become its counsellors. Men of mature age, and ripe experience, are set aside as too *slow*. Indeed, power passes from men, to women, and boys; and not to the women who veil their faces and listen to the priest, but to women who, with brazen front, spout infidelity under the name of philanthropy or humanity, and bid us forget their sex, and treat them as men. The result will soon be seen."

CHAPTER XIII.

IN the evening after the last conversation, the metropolitan editor left us. Whether his duties called him away, or whether he had grown weary of the part he had played, I know not; but I am sure he left us no less and no more prejudiced against the Church, no less and no more firm in his belief in the nineteenth century, than before. The priest had made not the slightest impression on his mind. The whole had been for him a sparring match. He did justice to the priest's skill in fence, admired it, and that was all. The priest's words had by no means convinced me, for I could not come at once to look favorably on the Church that I had been accustomed, from earliest childhood, to regard as the Mystery of Iniquity, the Sorceress of Babylon, the Mother of Abominations. Had I not been taught that the Pope is Anti-Christ, the veritable Man of Sin,—that the Church had apostatized, fallen away from Christ, corrupted the faith, imbruted the nations, and left the worship of the living and true God for the worship of idols, graven images, senseless pictures, and dead men's bones?

It is true, that as I had grown older, and traveled abroad in Catholic as well as in Protestant countries, this early teaching had lost with me much of its sharpness, and been not a little modified; yet the early impression it made on my mind remained, and prevented me from even examining, as I might have done, the practical effects of the doctrine and practices of the Church on the members of her communion who really believed her teaching, obeyed her precepts, and practised her morality. The aged priest, at our little watering-place of Springdale, was the first Catholic of whose inner life I had ever caught even the faintest glimpse.

I saw in this meek and modest old man, a man of learning and ability, born to a princely title and vast estates, brought up in wealth and luxury, highly cultivated and refined, foregoing all, making himself poor by his charities, leaving rank and family, country and friends, becoming a hard-working missionary in a foreign land, among a people strangers in speech, manners, and blood, the great majority of whom looked upon his religion with bitter hatred, and upon himself as an emissary of Satan, and where there were only a widely-scattered few who would recognize his sacred calling, ask his services, and who were in general poor and despised, the pariahs of society. With these he had spent, without murmuring or repining, in cheerfulness and gaiety of heart, forty of the best years of his life, in journeyings from place to place, lodging in miserable shanties, sometimes on the bare ground, teaching the ignorant, consoling the afflicted, recalling the erring, rebuking the sinner, visiting the sick and dying, and burying the dead; often in hunger and thirst, in watchings and fastings, and ready to faint from weariness and exhaustion, and yet never counting his labor and want, his privations, and fatigue, holding himself repaid, and more than repaid, if so be he could win souls to Christ, and save his own soul at last. When I saw this, and reflected that he had done only what thousands had done before him, and were still doing, in all parts of the world, I could not but say to myself there must be something deeper and diviner in this old Church than we Protestants have believed possible.

The priest resolutely maintained, in some conversations I had with him after the editor had left us, that, except in the material order, due in great measure to the previous discovery by Catholics of this western hemisphere, and in the further extension and practical application of certain great principles always insisted on by the Church, there had been no real progress of civilization since the epoch of the Reformation. There was a great political and social change in Europe in the fifteenth century, he said, when monarchical centralism triumphed over feudalism which had reigned for four centuries; but whether the change was a progress or not, many students of history and society think is quite doubtful. The change, as far as he had been able to understand it, consisted, he said, in principle at least, in a return to what may be called the Græco-Roman order of civilization, which had been weakened but not destroyed by the Barbarian invasion of the Empire. The change has certainly been in favor of monarchy, and, in the more advanced nations of Europe, has resulted in the reestablishment of Cæsarism.

The struggle now going on in Europe, the echo of which affects the American system most disastrously, he said, is the attempt to substitute democratic absolutism for monarchical absolutism, as it was in England during what is called the English Rebellion in the seventeenth century, and in the French Revolution in the eighteenth, not yet ended. The party of democratic absolutism is regarded, just now, as the party of progress, the party of thé future, the party of humanity, and because it represents the spirit of the age and promises the race unbounded liberty and an earthly paradise. What favors it is approved; what opposes it is condemned. Would you oppose the people, pit yourself against your age, and repress its aspirations? Yet both absolutisms are founded on a falsehood, for they are founded on man, and man, either individually or collectively, is not absolute, but dependent and relative.

"But Liberalism is the great word of the day No human institution is strong enough to resist it, and it would, if it were possible, sweep away the Divine. Its force is the force of passion, not reason. You began your movement by rejecting the authority of the Pope and Councils, and asserting that of the Bible interpreted by private illumination or by private judgment, and have gone on and denied the authority of the Bible, and asserted, first, that of the interior spirit, and then, that of reason alone. You have been forced, by the light of your Liberal movement, to go farther, and reject the interior spirit, to reason and to restrict yourselves to the senses, and finally to the passions and instincts of the people. You have lost faith, lost hope in another world, resolved God into man, and man into a mere animal—probably the tadpole or monkey developed. To this you have been forced, step after step, and you call it progress! You have got rid of the spiritual order, emancipated what you regard as the advanced portion of mankind—the only portion in your estimation worth counting—from the restraints of all law except the physical laws of your constitution and those of the universe; have discarded all moral ideals as vain illusions, and are reduced, naked and alone, to your own passions and lusts. You have proclaimed people-king, people-priest, people-God, and made popular opinion, fickle as the wind, your law, your criterion of right and wrong. Under your progress in losing, poverty increases in greater ratio than wealth, the poor become more and more abject and servile, and are treated as unfortunates or criminals. Intelligence is lowered, minds lose their vigor, characters are enfeebled and abased, and man loses his dignity, his personal freedom and independence.

"Yet you applaud yourselves for the wonderful progress you have made, and for your immeasurable superiority over the generations that went before you. The evils to which we call your attention, and which you were told beforehand would inevitably follow your course, you excuse as the necessary incidents of the transition state through which you are passing, and trust they will disappear when you have left the Old completely behind, and have fully established the New. Alas! you are always in a transition state. You started from passion, not reason; from falsehood, not truth; from a false not a true principle; and how can you expect to arrive at anything fixed, solid, and permanent? You are following an illusion, a will-o'-the-wisp, and can hardly escape being caught in the bogs, or sunk in the quagmire at last.

"You were warned in the beginning of the danger you run, of the inevitable consequences of the false principle you adopted, and you called those who told you the truth, and begged you to heed their words, 'fools' and 'asses.' Even to-day you mock at us who try to rend the veil from your eyes, dispel your illusions, and enable you to see things as they are; you get angry at us, abuse us, call us moral cowards, dwellers among the tombs, worshipers of the dead past, with our eyes on the back side of our heads, lovers of darkness and haters of light, deniers of God and enemies of man. We are your enemies, forsooth, because we tell you the truth, and insist that it is truth, not error, that gives freedom to the mind, strength and energy to reason, elevation and dignity to character.

"The Church has always and everywhere," he continued, "had to struggle with the world, and always and everywhere will you find much, even in Catholic countries, to deplore; for never yet, even in professedly Catholic states, have the evil passions and ignorance of statesmen, and the blindness and ambition of rulers left her an open field and fair play. The Philistines, moreover, have always continued to dwell in the land. Yet you must have been struck in your travels with the moral elevation and personal dignity of the Catholic peasantry, and their freedom from the debasing servility to rank and wealth, from which the poor are not by any means free even in democratic America. The poor in Catholic countries are never abject as a class, and retain, even when beggars, a certain self-respect, personal dignity, and independence of feeling. They feel that

'A man's a man for a' that.'

Compare a Spanish or an Irish peasant with an English peasant, and my meaning is at once apparent. Did it ever occur to you that this superior moral elevation and personal dignity and independence of the Catholic poor are due to their religion, which attaches merit to voluntary poverty, regards the poor as blest and a blessing, and never treats them as an unfortunate class, or poverty as an evil, far less as a crime? These modern bastiles, called poor-houses, in which the poor are shut up as criminals, are not Catholic constructions, and I think you have never seen in Catholic countries, as I have in this country, the poor set up at auction in town-meeting, and knocked down to the lowest bidder, or person who would take and keep them at the least expense to the town. In Catholic states public charities and corrections are seldom classed together and placed in charge of one and the same board of commissioners.

"There was no little barbarism in the temper and manners of what are called 'the Dark Ages,' inherited from pagan Rome even more than from the German barbarian; but you will look in vain among your non-Catholic contemporaries for that clearness and vigor of intellect, and that moral elevation, force, and independence of individual character, which you meet everywhere in mediæval society. If there were great crimes in those ages, they were followed, as the historian of the Monks of the West justly remarks, by grand expiations. If there was great pride, there was deeper humility, and always will the period from the sixth to the end of the fifteenth century stand out as the most glorious in the annals of the race.

"The movement party curses those ages, and for a century and a half has been engaged in a huge leveling process, which, while it has done really nothing to elevate the depressed, and has really injured the poor by multiplying their wants, and aggravating their discontent, has brought down all elevations to the low level of commonplace. The progress you boast consists chiefly in losing the rich faith, the high principle, the elevated character, and the sublime ideal cherished by the Church, and in reducing all moral, intellectual, individual, and social eminences to a general average, where the race stagnates and rots."

I will not say the priest was right, that he did not exaggerate, or even adopt a false rule of judgment; but I felt that he had thought longer and far more deeply on the subject than I had.

He had evidently mastered the subject to a degree, and studied it in a light that I had not done, and I had no right to regard him as less honest and truthful, or more "one-sided" than myself. He made me feel I knew very little of the real history of my race—that I had frittered away my time, and that there were depths and analogies even in common things that I had not dreamed of exploring. He showed me at least that I had many things as to the principles and influence of religion and the Church: to learn, and stimulated me to do all in my power at any age to redeem the time I had lost.

I do not think I shall ever be convinced of the priest's doctrine, and seek admission into the communion of the Catholic Church; but I am thoroughly resolved to investigate, if my life is prolonged, her claims, which I am certain are not as unreasonable or as unfounded as I had hitherto supposed.

THE END

www.ingramcontent.com/pod-product-compliance
Lightning Source LLC
Chambersburg PA
CBHW050808160426
43192CB00010B/1683